THE NATIONAL TRUST
BOOK OF PICNICS

In the same series

THE NATIONAL TRUST BOOK OF PICNICS

Compiled by

Kate Crookenden, Caroline Worlledge
and Margaret Willes

THE NATIONAL TRUST

ISBN 0 7078 0158 3

Copyright © The National Trust 1993

First published in Great Britain in 1993 by
National Trust Enterprises Limited
36 Queen Anne's Gate
London SW1H 9AS

Registered charity number 205846

British Library Cataloguing-in-Publication Data.
A catalogue record for this book is available from
the British Library.

Illustrations by John Finnie

Designed by Gail Engert

Phototypeset in Monotype Lasercomp Times 327
by Southern Positives and Negatives (SPAN),
Lingfield, Surrey (8995)

Printed in England by
Butler & Tanner Ltd, Frome, Somerset

CONTENTS

ACKNOWLEDGEMENTS

We would like to thank the following for their help with this book: Simone Sekers for recipes, advice and her opinions on picnics of yore; Sara Paston-Williams, for information that she has generously given us from her book, *The Art of Dining: A History of Cooking and Eating* (to be published autumn 1993); Jackie Gurney for use of material from the first version of *The National Trust Book of Picnics*; and our many regional colleagues for their help and support.

The Publishers are grateful to the following for permission to use material; HarperCollins Publishers for the excerpt from *English Picnics* by Georgina Battiscombe, Harvill Press, 1949, and Terence Dalton Ltd for the excerpt from *Courtsy to the Lady* by Zoë Ward, Terence Dalton, 1985.

CONVERSIONS

The following approximate conversions are used in this book.

$\frac{1}{4}$ oz	7 g	$2\frac{3}{4}$ fluid oz	75 ml
$\frac{1}{2}$ oz	15 g	4 fluid oz	100 ml
1 oz	25 g	5 fluid oz	125 ml
$1\frac{1}{2}$ oz	40 g	$\frac{1}{4}$ pint	150 ml
2 oz	50 g	$\frac{1}{3}$ pint	200 ml
$2\frac{1}{2}$ oz	65 g	$\frac{1}{2}$ pint	300 ml
3 oz	75 g	12 fluid oz	350 ml
$3\frac{1}{2}$ oz	100 g	$\frac{3}{4}$ pint	450 ml
4 oz	125 g	1 pint	600 ml
5 oz	150 g	$1\frac{1}{2}$ pints	900 ml
6 oz	175 g	2 pints	1.2 litres
7 oz	200 g	8 pints	4.5 litres
8 oz	225 g		
9 oz	250 g		
10 oz	275 g		
12 oz	350 g		
14 oz	400 g		
15 oz	435 g		
1 lb	450 g	275°F	140°C	gas mark 1
$1\frac{1}{4}$ lb	550 g	300°F	150°C	2
$1\frac{1}{2}$ lb	675 g	325°F	160°C	3
$1\frac{3}{4}$ lb	800 g	350°F	180°C	4
$2\frac{1}{4}$ lb	1 kg	375°F	190°C	5
$2\frac{1}{2}$ lb	1125 g	400°F	200°C	6
3 lb	1.4 kg	425°F	220°C	7
4 lb	1.8 kg	450°F	230°C	8

AMERICAN EQUIVALENTS

Information very kindly provided by the Good Housekeeping Institution

Dry Measures

1 US cup	=	50g	=	2oz of: breadcrumbs; fresh cake crumbs
1 US cup	=	75g	=	3oz of: rolled oats
1 US cup	=	90g	=	3½ oz of: desiccated coconut; ground almonds
1 US cup	=	100g	=	4oz of: suet; grated hard cheese; walnut pieces; drinking chocolate; sugar; cocoa; flaked almonds; pasta; frozen peas
1 US cup	=	125g	=	5oz of: white flour; self-raising flour; currants; muesli; chopped dates; ground roasted almonds
1 US cup	=	150g	=	5½oz of: wholemeal flour; raisins; cornflour
1 US cup	=	175g	=	6oz of: apricots; mixed peel; sultanas
1 US cup	=	200g	=	7oz of: caster sugar; soft brown sugar; demerara sugar; glacé cherries; lentils; long grain and brown rice; flaked and drained tuna fish
1 US cup	=	225g	=	½lb of: cream cheese; cottage cheese
1 US cup	=	300g	=	11oz of: mincemeat; marmalade
1 US cup	=	350g	=	12oz of: syrup; treacle; jam

Liquid Measures

¼ US cup	=	60ml	=	2 fluid oz
1 US cup	=	240ml	=	8 fluid oz
2 US cups (1 US pint)	=	480ml	=	16 fluid oz

Butter, Lard and Margarine Measures

¼ stick	=	25g	=	2 level tablespoons	=	1oz
1 stick (½ US cup)	=	100g	=	8 level tablespoons	=	4oz

INTRODUCTION

INTRODUCTION

A picnic is the Englishman's grand gesture, his final defiance flung
in the face of fate . . . [he] refuses to frequent an outdoor cafe of any
sort, obstinately clinging to his picnic basket in wet and wasp-
haunted fields.

Georgina Battiscombe, *English Picnics*, 1949

In September 1992, when friends wished to remember the great
cookery writer Elizabeth David, they chose to follow her memorial
service in London with a picnic. Why is the picnic such a British
tradition? It seems an odd phenomenon considering the vagaries of our
weather. Or perhaps it represents the triumph of hope over adversity.

And where did this fascination for picnics spring from? The word first
makes its appearance in England in one of the letters of advice written
by Lord Chesterfield to his son. On 29 October 1748 he wrote: 'I like the
description of your picnic, where I take it for granted that your cards
are only to break the formality of the circle, and your symposium
intended more to promote conversation than drinking.' I fear that Lord
Chesterfield's assumptions about the temperance of picnics were not
well founded.

Half a century later, *The Times* provided a succinct definition of what
was meant by a picnic. On 18 March 1802 it reported: 'A picnic supper
consists of a variety of dishes. The subscriber to the entertainment has
the bill of fare presented to them with a number against each dish. The
lot which he draws obliges him to furnish the dish marked against it,
which he either takes with him in his carriage or sends by a servant.' In
other words, Georgian picnics were rather like the modern idea of a
shared dinner party where guests contribute courses.

In the same year as *The Times'* notice, a Picnic Club was founded by
Lady Buckinghamshire and Lady Jersey, chatelaine of Osterley Park in
Middlesex. Other members included the Prince of Wales and his
mistress and secret wife, Mrs Fitzherbert. The inaugural meeting
consisted of private theatricals at Tottenham Street Rooms in London,
followed by a picnic supper in a tavern. Although one member protested
it was a 'harmless and inoffensive society of persons of fashion', the
Morning Herald thought otherwise: 'it being apprehended that the
public peace might be disturbed by this irregular assemblage, the Bow
Street officers held themselves in readiness to act during the whole
evening . . .'. The cartoonists weighed in too, with Gillray depicting 'The

13

Picnic Orchestra' with a prodigiously stout Lady Buckinghamshire at the piano and Lady Salisbury blowing a hunting horn. The Club proved to be short-lived, closing down in February 1803.

Other long-standing British eating traditions combined with this concept to produce the picnic that we know and love today. Georgina Battiscombe has, with great ingenuity, come up with the earliest recorded picnic, an Anglo-Saxon tale written down in the Chronicle of Reginald, a monk of Durham, in the ninth century. Some time between 875 and 883, the monks of Lindisfarne had fled to the Northumbrian mainland to escape the Danes, taking with them the body of St Cuthbert. Sheltering somewhere near Hadrian's Wall, they were provided with sustenance by the local community. One gift was a freshly made cheese, which proved too much of a temptation for one monk, Eilaf. His companions didn't notice their loss until they were having a picnic of salted horse's head and felt the need to relieve the monotony with some cheese. Outcry followed, and a curse, 'May Holy Cuthbert grant us that the thief of his and our cheese may become a little fox.' Eilaf duly turned into a fox with the cheese in his mouth. After his fellow monks had had a good laugh at his expense, further exhortations reverted him to his monastic being, though he was thereafter always known as Brother Tod.

One ancestor of the picnic was the hunting feast, enjoyed by the rich and privileged in medieval and Tudor times. A hunting treatise, *Le Livre de la Chasse*, written by Gaston de Foix in 1387, was translated as *Master of the Game* by Edward, Duke of York, cousin to Henry V and one of the few English nobles to be killed at the Battle of Agincourt. Before this unlucky end, he set down the ideal site for a feast: 'The place where the gathering shall be made shall be in a fair mead, well green, where fair trees grow all about, the one far from the other, or beside some running brook... They that come from home shall bring thither all they need, every one in his office, well and plenteously, and set diverse meats in great plenty.'

The Gaston de Foix of the Elizabethan court was George Turbeville with his *Noble Art of Venerie*, printed in 1575. He ensured he was in the royal good books by reproducing a woodcut of Elizabeth I attending a hunt breakfast. He lists in verse the dishes to be enjoyed by the Royal party before the hunt:

For whiles colde loynes of veale, cold capon, beefe and goose
With pygeon pyes, and mutton colde, are set on hunger loose
First neates [ox] tongues poudred well, and gambones of the hogge
Then sausages and savery knackes, to set mens myndes on gogge

After the kill, the Tudor equivalent of a barbecue was set up: 'some fine seauce made with wine and spices in a fair dish upon a chafing dish and coals, to the end that as he or she doth behold the huntsman breaking up the deer, they may take their pleasure of the sweet dainty morsels and dress some of them on the coals, making carbonadoes.'

Hunting lodges were often built so that the chase could be watched under cover, and the feast enjoyed even in inclement weather. Newark Park in Gloucestershire was built in the mid-sixteenth century by the courtier Sir Nicholas Poyntz as a hunting 'stand', and other examples can be seen at Chatsworth in Derbyshire, built for Bess of Hardwick, and at Sherborne in Gloucestershire.

From the hunting feast descended the shooting luncheon, so much enjoyed by Victorians. The gentlemen with their guns, their ladies, the gun loaders and the beaters all had to be catered for. In fine weather, trestle tables were set up; otherwise a table would be laid in the gamekeeper's cottage. The butler and footmen would serve up to the gentry casseroles, game pies and hams; suet and plum puddings, apple pies and dumplings; plum cake and cheese. For drinks there would be wine, beer and cider, sloe gin and cherry brandy. The loaders were provided with big hot joints of meat and hot potatoes, the beaters, bread and cheese, all served with beer.

The Prince Consort was an enthusiastic shot and Queen Victoria's *Leaves from the Journal of our Life in the Highlands* often describes shooting picnics, though of a more spartan nature than the one just mentioned. On 6 October 1857, 'At 12 o'clock I drove off with the girls to the "irons", where we mounted our ponies, and rode up ([John] Brown and Robertson attending on foot) through the *Corrie Buie*, along the pretty new path through *Feithluie* to the foot of the very steep ascent to *Feithort*, where we got off and walked up – and suddenly, when nearly at the top of the path, came upon Albert's little encampment, which was just at the edge of the winding path. Albert was still absent, having gone out at 6 o'clock, but Lohlein and some of the gillies were there. The little house, with shelves for keeping some boxes (no seat), and a little stove, was not at all uncomfortable; but the wind was dreadfully high, and blew in ... We lunched in the little "housie" at the open door.'

Another ancestor of the picnic was the banquet. In the Middle Ages, Tudor and Stuart times, this did not mean a great feast, as it might today, but applied to a final course at the end of a meal. Dinner usually consisted of two main courses, with all the dishes, savoury and sweet, served up together. For special occasions and for honoured guests, an extra course would be offered, like a dessert, after the table had been cleared, or in a completely separate room, or even a separate building. Lacock Abbey in Wiltshire was owned in the mid-sixteenth century by Sir William Sharington, a protégé of Lord Protector Somerset and *au fait* with the latest fashions. In an octagonal tower at Lacock he served banquets on an exquisite classical stone table: both tower and table can be visited today. At Hardwick Hall in Derbyshire, Bess of Hardwick would have provided banquets for guests in little rooms on the flat roof of her magnificent house, so that they might also enjoy the views of the surrounding countryside, or in a little pavilion in the garden. The lovely little garden pavilions at Montacute in Somerset are also thought to have been used for banquets. At Lyveden in Northamptonshire, Sir Thomas Tresham planned to build a whole house, the New Bield, for summer banquets.

The food eaten at these banquets was usually sweet and rich. Jellies, tarts, fruit conserves and marmalades, marchpane (marzipan), ginger-bread, comfits, and exotically named suckets and codiniacs, were prepared in the still-room by the lady of the house with her maids. If she found this to be too much of a chore, she could send out to specialist confectioners. A modern recipe which is redolent of banqueting stuff is Simone Sekers's delicious *panforte* given on p.33.

The ancestor of the picnic as moveable feast is food for travellers. It is almost impossible for us to imagine how difficult travel must have been in medieval England. All through the winter, even the greatest highways were rendered impassable by bad weather, and whole communities could be cut off for months on end. So it must have been thrilling at springtime to be able to move around again; hence Chaucer's cele-bration of April showers at the beginning of *The Canterbury Tales*. Froissart, the fourteenth-century chronicler, was likewise lyrical in his poem, *Espritte Amoureuse*. This is set in France, but May Day was similarly observed by the English: 'In the First day of jolly May – God how fair was the season! – the air was clear and windless and serene, and the nightingales sang aloud, and we came to a thorn bush all white with blossom; lance-high it stood, with fair, green shade underneath... Then with one accord we brought out the meats, pasties, hams, wines and bakemeats [pies], and venison packed in heather.' The heather packing is believed to be a reference to a kind of haybox arrangement to keep the meat hot in transit, just as one might use newspaper wrapping in a similar way today.

Samuel Pepys was a great picnicker. His diaries refer to meals taken on the move in his carriage. With his interest in the navy, he would often spend the day on the lower reaches of the Thames, watching the ships at anchor and having a water party. His diary for 6 July 1664 records: 'Up very betimes, and my wife also, and got us ready; and about eight o'clock, having got some bottles of wine and beer and neats' tongues, we went to our barge at the Tower [of London], where Mr Pierce and his wife and a kinswoman and his sister, and Mrs Clerke and her sister and cousin were to expect us. And so set out for the Hope [the reach of the river downstream from Tilbury], all the way down playing at Cards and other sports, spending our time pretty merry. Came to the Hope about one, and there showed them all the ships and had a collacion of anchovies, Gammon, etc, and so to cards and other sports till we came to Greenwich.'

Another shrewd observer of the contemporary scene was John Byng, Lord Torrington, whose journals cover the years 1781 to 1792. Whereas Pepys's excursions were made mostly within London and its environs, Byng loved to travel further afield. In a sense he was godfather to today's National Trust visitor. Every summer he would take a vacation from his job as a civil servant in the Inland Revenue office to go sightseeing in England or Wales. In his delightful journals, details of meals at inns are lovingly recorded – good ones and bad ones – but there is only one reference to a picnic. This took place on 13 June 1792 when Byng was visiting the High Force Waterfall in Middleton-in-Teesdale in Yorkshire:

> I am here in that sort of wild country and unvisited village that I wish to explore, and wherein to lose the memory of all the midnight follies and extravagant foolish conversation of the capital. From Barnard Castle it is reckoned ten miles to this place, which I rode in three hours and a half. Trembling for their roads and miles, I had brought a nightcap in my pocket. Having ordered dinner, hired a guide and crammed his and Garwood's pocket with bread, cheese and ale (brandy I idly forgot), we resumed our march.
> ... We crept through the boggy wood into the field, where opening our budget like Lord North, we ate and drank voraciously, I walking about for my head was as wet as my feet.

After this miserable day, Byng was thankful to be back at the inn, dining on roasted fillet of beef, potatoes and the local speciality of potted trout. Reunited with his liquor, 'My head I rubbed with brandy, with some of the half pint I quickly finished.'

Byng clearly lacked the Wordsworths' hardiness. Dorothy's journals are full of descriptions of picnics in the Lake District, winter and summer. One particularly harrowing example was taken in January 1802 by William, Dorothy and Mary Hutchinson, William's future wife: nobody could have accused the last of not knowing what she was letting herself in for. Bound for Grasmere, they rejected the high road over Kirkstone Pass, choosing instead the short but difficult track over Grisedale Hause. Even on this bitter winter day, a picnic was taken of ham, bread and milk, before starting on a path with 'no footmark upon the snow either of man or beast' and nearly ending the expedition in disaster.

A more enjoyable picnic was eaten to celebrate victory at the Battle of Waterloo. On 21 August 1815, the Wordsworths and Robert Southey were amongst a group that climbed Skiddaw to light 'a joyful bonfire'. Arriving at the top, they had roast beef, plum pudding and punch, singing *God Save the King* round a bonfire made of tar barrels, before rolling blazing balls of tar and turpentine down the mountainside.

One of the earliest fictional accounts of an English picnic comes in Jane Austen's *Emma*, published in 1816. An excursion is proposed to the Surrey beauty spot of Box Hill, with a cold collation of lamb and pigeon pies 'to be done in a quiet, unpretending, elegant way, infinitely superior to the bustle and preparation, the regular eating and drinking and picnic parade of the Eltons and Sucklings.' But plans go awry, and in the event there are two excursions, one to Donwell Abbey to take advantage of the strawberries there, with a debate as to whether the lunch should be taken in or out of doors. The following day, the picnic does take place at Box Hill, but is not a success: 'During the whole two hours that were spent on the Hill there seemed a principle of separation between the other parties, too strong for any fine prospects, or any cold collation . . . to remove.' After the 'very questionable enjoyments of the day of pleasure', Emma returns home in tears.

The final ancestor of the picnic is the communal celebration. The medieval concept of hospitality encouraged the lord of the manor to provide feasts in celebration of high days and holidays for his neighbours, rich and poor. The Twelve Days of Christmas were particularly an opportunity for feasting, very welcome to the poor, whose diet must have been at its most frugal at this time of the year. These Christmas feasts continued through the centuries. At Wallington in Northumberland at the end of the nineteenth century, Lady Trevelyan would give an end-of-year party where Christmas beef – 4lb for a single man, 6lb for a couple, and 1lb for every child – was distributed to all estate employees and their dependants.

The coming of age of the heir to the estate was often a chance for great public feasting. One party that got hopelessly out of hand was the celebration of the twenty-first birthday of Lord Hartington, heir to the Duke of Devonshire, held in May 1811 for the tenantry and neighbouring peasantry of Hardwick Hall. William Howitt, a Quaker, walked over from Mansfield to watch the scene. To his horror, he came upon a man in the park, lying under a tree, dead drunk. As he got closer to the house, so the number of prone bodies increased. Cascades of ale were spurting from barrels, to be caught by revellers in their hats. At the garden gates, servants acting as bouncers tried to repel gatecrashers by thumping them over the head with staves, but to little effect. In the house itself, Howitt found scores of people eating chunks of roast beef and plum pudding off pewter dishes, and drinking from leather jacks and tankards. Those still outside demanded food, whereupon meat and pudding were hurled out of the window. Worse was to come – two men were killed as a wall collapsed. This proved too much for William Howitt, who left the scene, determined to return on a more tranquil occasion.

A more disciplined public feast was provided by the 3rd Earl Egremont of Petworth in Sussex. On his birthday in December he would hold a huge party for his estate workers, their wives and children. In 1834, however, he was too ill on his birthday, so a picnic was held the following May. The scene was captured in paint by William Witherington in a picture still hanging at Petworth, and in words by the diarist Charles Greville:

> ... a fine sight it was: fifty-four tables, each fifty feet long, were placed in a vast semi-circle on the lawn before the house. Nothing could be more amusing than to look at the preparations. The tables were all spread with cloths, and plates, and dishes; two great tents were erected in the middle to receive the provisions, which were conveyed in carts, like ammunition. Plum puddings and loaves were piled like cannon-balls, and innumerable joints of boiled and roast beef were spread out, while hot joints were prepared in the kitchen, and sent forth as soon as the firing of the guns announced the hour of the feast. Tickets were given to the inhabitants of a certain district, and the number was about 4000; but, as many more came, the Old Peer could not endure that there should be anybody hungering outside the gates, and he went out himself and ordered the barriers to be taken down and admittance given to all. They think 6000 were fed. Gentlemen from the neighbourhood carved for them, and waiters were provided from among the peasantry.

Fireworks ended a day on which 10,000 people were said to have assembled. One thousand yards of table-cloth were bought for the occasion, plus eleven hundred stone of meat and a thousand plum puddings.

Most Victorian picnics were not on this gargantuan scale. Nevertheless, they required a large amount of organisation if Mrs Beeton had anything to do with it. In her *Book of Household Management* of 1861 she devotes pages to the subject. She advises on what to eat: for 40 persons, a rib of cold roast beef, a joint of cold boiled beef, 2 ribs of lamb, 4 roast fowls, 2 roast ducks, 1 ham, 1 tongue, 2 veal-and-ham pies, 2 pigeon pieces, 6 medium-sized lobsters, 1 piece of collared calves head, 18 lettuces, 6 baskets of salad, 6 cucumbers; stewed fruit well sweetened and put into glass bottles well corked, 3 or 4 dozen plain pastry biscuits to eat with fruit, 2 dozen fruit turnovers, 4 dozen cheese cakes, 2 cold cabinet puddings in moulds, a few jam puffs, 1 large cold Christmas pudding (this must be good), a few baskets of fresh fruit,

3 dozen plain biscuits, a piece of cheese, 6lbs of butter (this, of course includes the butter for tea – [tea!], 4 quartern loaves of household bread, 3 dozen rolls, 6 loaves of tin bread (for tea), 2 plain plum cakes, 2 pound cakes, 2 sponge cakes, a tin of mixed biscuits, ½lb of tea. She adds that coffee is not suitable, being difficult to make.

Moving on to the beverages, Mrs Beeton advises: 3 dozen quart bottles of ale, ginger beer, soda-water and lemonade, of each 2 dozen bottles, 6 bottles of sherry, 6 bottles of claret, champagne at discretion and any other light wine that may be preferred, and 2 bottles of brandy. 'Water can usually be obtained, so it is useless to take it.'

Nothing could be left to chance. Mrs Beeton then explores *Things not to be Forgotten at a Picnic*. An odd miscellany follows: 'a stick of horseradish, a bottle of good mint sauce well corked, a bottle of salad dressing, a bottle of vinegar, made mustard, pepper, salt, good oil and pounded sugar ... It is scarcely necessary to say that plates, tumblers, wine glasses, knives, forks and spoons must not be forgotten, as also teacups and saucers, 3 or 4 teapots, some lump sugar and milk, if this article cannot be obtained in the neighbourhood. Take three cork-screws.'

Finally Mrs Beeton provides handy tips for the hostess: 'Provided care has been taken in choosing congenial guests, and that in a mixed party one sex does not predominate, a well-arranged picnic is one of the pleasantest forms of entertainment. Watch carefully not to provide too much of one thing and too little of another; avoid serving plenty of salad and no dressing; two or three legs of mutton and no mint sauce; an abundance of wine and no corkscrew. Given a happy party of young people, bent on enjoyment, these are trifles light as air, which serve rather to increase the fun than to diminish it. But, on the other hand, the party may not all be young and merry; it may be very distasteful to some to have to suffer these inconveniences.'

This kind of meal could only be contemplated by those with an abundance of time, money and servants. But other moves were afoot. The Bank Holiday Act of 1871 made it possible for all working men and women to consider taking a day, if not a week, away. The development of the railways, the introduction of comfortable bicycles, and later the invention of the motor car all made the idea of travel attractive without the necessity for a great deal of wealth. But most of the food so far described – the joints of meat and plum puddings so dear to the British heart – are not easily transportable. Apart from that modest perennial, bread and cheese, and pies and pasties, most moveable food comes from hotter climes like the Mediterranean, as can be seen in the recipes in this book. The one supreme exception to this is the sandwich – born not of the bracing outdoor meal, but in the smoke-filled gambling room. John Montagu, 4th Earl of Sandwich, was so loath to leave the gaming table that he got his valet to provide him with sustenance in the form of a slice of cold roast beef between two pieces of bread.

The sandwich, which has become such an ubiquitous feature of picnics, rouses extremes of emotion. To Sir Osbert Sitwell it was an abomination. In his essay, *Picnics & Pavilions*, he likens the sandwich to 'slimy layers of paste like something out of the Ancient Mariner

> "... O Christ!
> That ever this should be!
> Yea, slimy things did crawl with legs
> Upon the slimy sea".'

Beachcomber in the *Daily Telegraph*, on the other hand, remembers dryness as the overriding quality. Of the British railway sandwiches of yore, he remarked, 'They are taken out each day and dusted in order of seniority'.

Sir John Betjeman in his poem, *Trebetherick*, evokes the memory that many of us have for picnics held at the seaside: 'Sand in the sandwiches, wasps in the tea.' But for Simone Sekers the sandwich of our childhood brings back pure bliss. In a teasing piece published in the *Sunday Telegraph* on 16 August 1992, she recalls fondly the sandwiches of the 1950s: 'sandwich spread and bacon, peanut butter (crunchy) and home-made plum jam – even plain black treacle on occasion. Hard-boiled egg was popular, especially when married to salad cream (the terrible hair-oil mayonnaise hadn't been invented then).'

I have to say that my memories of picnics of that era are not as happy as hers. Patient negotiations preceded the selection of the ideal site, with silent resentment from those outvoted. Any spot selected was bound to conceal lurking dangers, like cow-pats, thistles, or an infestation of wasps or ants. Salad cream, and worse, sandwich spread, were an anthema to me; so too was the plastic flavour imparted to hot drinks by the mugs. Thus, unlike Simone, I am thrilled by the advent of bottled 'hair-oil' mayonnaise, padded cushions, ice-boxes, mobile barbecues and expendable cups and glasses, and feel that picnics have undergone a wondrous revival in the past few years.

This would seem to be the opinion of National Trust picnickers too. Visitors are welcome to picnic at many properties, and a list of ones that are particularly appropriate is provided at the back of this book. But bear in mind the cautionary tale of one National Trust donor. So infuriated was she at the sight of people picnicking on her lawns, she took note of the car registration, tracked down the picnickers' address, and duly returned the compliment – in their small front garden! So, if there is a sign requesting not to picnic, please respect it. There are usually plenty of alternatives.

The National Trust also provides the venue for wonderful communal picnics, *fêtes champêtres*, held every summer. They seem to work most successfully in the great eighteenth-century landscape gardens like Claremont, Stourhead, West Wycombe and Stowe, and have become very much a feature of the National Trust summer season. Here, picnickers are at their most resourceful, with tables and chairs carefully transported alongside the ice-box and the hampers, with hurricane lamps and even candelabra as the finishing touch.

Whether you are having a daytime picnic, or attending a *fête champêtre*, raise a glass to all those shadowy picnickers from the past: Brother Tod on Hadrian's Wall, Bess of Hardwick in her banqueting house, Lord Egremont catering for ten thousand at Petworth, and Wordsworth and Southey joining hands on top of Skiddaw.

Margaret Willes
Publisher

TRAVELLING
PICNICS

TRAVELLING PICNICS

T he medieval ruins of Fountains Abbey in Yorkshire form a romantic backdrop to the great eighteenth-century landscape garden of Studley Royal. Visitors have flocked to Fountains and Studley for nearly three centuries. This American visitor, writing home in a letter dated 15 September 1839, describes a picnic taken there:

> [We] went in a postchaise, a postboy in red on one of the horses, ... started in the morning, took two baskets containing partridge pie, roast lamb, six tarts, cake, bread and butter, soda water, Ale, Champagne, and porter ... we took our walk over the ground before dinner ... once in a while we would say, 'Cousin William, do you think we brought enough provision?' I think I was never so hungrey [sic] in my life. I think you would have enjoyed the ramble exceedingly and I am quite sure the dinner after it, which we took in a building provided for visitors.

Alan Bennett sets Fountains Abbey as the goal for a bicycle outing in his play, *A Day Out*. The year is 1911, and the members of the Halifax Cycling Club, gentlemen only, have set off for the day. Arriving at the Abbey, the group have their picnic of sandwiches and fruit before scattering to indulge in wildly different activities: taking a sedate historical tour, playing cricket among the medieval ruins, getting involved in a croquet party at the big house, and seducing the local lasses.

A very different kind of travelling picnic is described in Arthur Ransome's *Swallows and Amazons*, published in 1930. It is believed that Captain Flint's houseboat, which plays a vital role in the book, was based by Ransome on the steam yacht *Gondola*. This yacht, first launched in 1859 to carry passengers from the Furness Railway Company across Coniston Water in the Lake District, still plies the waters of the lake and is now in the care of the National Trust. Sadly, the victory picnic provided by Captain Flint is not on offer on *Gondola*:

> It was as good a feast as Captain Flint had been able to get sent from Rio. For example, there were ices, strawberry ones. There were parkins and bath buns and rock cakes and ginger-nuts and chocolate biscuits. There were mountains of sandwiches to begin with. Then there was a cake with a paper cover over it. When the cover was lifted off, there was a picture of two little ships done in pink and white icing.

⬛ SANDWICHES ◪

No picnic book would be complete without a section on sandwiches. Although bread had long been used to serve food on or with, or as a shovel, we have to thank the 4th Earl of Sandwich in 1762 for 'putting the lid' on the sandwich so the filling was enclosed and he could eat his snack while gambling and not make the cards sticky! Sandwiches are traditional picnic fare and ideal for the travelling meal, leaving no waste bar the wrapper which is easily scrunched into a pocket until a litter bin is found.

Any bread can be used for a sandwich. There is nothing to stop you filling all kinds of bread – white, wholemeal, granary, rye, French sticks, baps, rolls, buns, pitta breads, croissants, bagels, to name but a few. If you are making a lot of sandwiches, bread made in a loaf tin, or bought in this shape, will make the most sandwiches. Although it is easier to butter one-day-old bread, there is nothing more delicious than really fresh bread with lots of filling.

If the list of breads available now seems exhaustive, the possible fillings for sandwiches are positively infinite and even to begin to list them would need a book in itself. The guidelines and suggestions below are intended as a starting point to inspire your own ideas for sandwich fillings.

Cold meat

It is much easier to eat a sandwich in which the meat has been chopped up or shredded rather than having to bite through the meat and leaving half behind to fall out of the sandwich! Use the same sauces to enhance the meat in the sandwich as you would on the table – horseradish or mustard for beef, mustard for ham, mint or redcurrant jelly for lamb, cranberry jelly or redcurrant for turkey or chicken. Chutneys of various kinds go well with cold meat, as do pickles and gherkins. Roast meats are mentioned below but pâté, corn beef, luncheon meat, pastrami, salamis and any others can be used in sandwiches with salads and mayonnaise.

Fish

Smoked salmon is a favourite for sandwiches; smoked trout or mackerel in flaked, sliced or pâté form are all good with a little horseradish. Taramasalata is easily spread in a sandwich and instead of smoked salmon, try using fresh. Prawns and shrimps are delicious with a little tomato purée or ketchup added to the mayonnaise, or sliced roll-mop herring with cream cheese and apple. For a very tasty sandwich, mix butter with anchovies and olives, blend and add tuna if required. Sardines and hard-boiled eggs chopped small with a little mayonnaise are also a good filling. All fish sandwiches will benefit from salad and mayonnaise.

Cheese

Hard cheeses can either be sliced or grated and are delicious spread with a fruit chutney. Only cream cheese has been used below, to avoid repetition, but low fat cream cheese or cottage cheese can be substituted in most cases. Brie has been used below, but any similar cheese such as camembert can be substituted.

Bacon

Small pieces of crispy bacon are best in sandwiches. These are achieved by using finely cut streaky bacon cooked to a crisp and then drained on kitchen towel. Do not keep for too long before using.

Salad

Lettuce, cucumber, tomato and spring onion can be added separately or together to most savoury sandwiches with a little mayonnaise. The cucumber and tomato should be thinly sliced, with the tomato seeds removed for smart picnics, and the lettuce shredded. Spring onion should be thinly sliced and used sparingly so as not to overwhelm the sandwich. Alternatively, use coleslaw, finely chopped potato or pasta salad. Salad sandwich on its own is delicious, or with potato or pasta salad and likewise coleslaw with pasta or potato salad.

Herbs

Finely chopped fresh herbs give wonderful flavour to a sandwich, especially chives, dill, parsley, mint, basil, rocket and coriander.

Eggs

Hard-boiled eggs are most commonly used in sandwiches, either thinly sliced or chopped up small and mixed with mayonnaise. Scrambled eggs, however, make a good sandwich, and fried or poached eggs with sausage or bacon are the ideal early start breakfast sandwich.

Making sandwiches

Sandwiches do not have to be two slices of bread with a filling, cut in halves or quarters. Other shapes and ways of constructing them are to make double or triple decker sandwiches, cut into fingers with different fillings between each layer.

Alternatively, for delicate bite-sized sandwiches, cut the loaf length-wise into slices, spread the filling and roll each slice up carefully starting from the long edge. At the picnic, cut the rolls into $\frac{1}{2}$-inch slices like a miniature Swiss roll.

For round loaves, try cutting the loaf in half around the waist making two discs. If it is very thick, slice off some slices from both cut edges and reserve these for making normal sandwiches. Scoop a little of the remaining soft bread out and place the filling, which should not be skimped and should be moist, on the bottom of the loaf, put on the top and cut in slices like a cake. With the slices cut off, make sandwiches and again, slice like a cake.

To get a thin and even spread of butter or margarine, start at the outside of the bread, not in the centre. Mayonnaise can be used as an alternative spread or in addition to keep the sandwich moist.

The sandwich will be better made as close to picnic time as possible, but if they have to be kept a long time, wrapping them in a damp cloth before packing them will prevent the bread drying out and curling. Wrap different flavours separately.

The suggestions that follow take a basic ingredient and then list various fillings which work well with it and in most cases with each other, so a combination of fillings can be used. Choose your favourites and mix them together.

Chicken or Turkey – salad, coleslaw, potato salad, pasta salad, curry mayonnaise, apricot or mango chutney, avocado, bacon, ham, sweetcorn, mayonnaise, cranberry sauce, redcurrant jelly, peanut butter, asparagus, prawns

Beef – horseradish, salad, coleslaw, mayonnaise, asparagus

Lamb – mint jelly, redcurrant jelly, salad, coleslaw, chutney, watercress

Ham – hard cheese, cottage cheese, brie, chutney, mustard, sweetcorn, mushroom, spinach, egg mayonnaise, pineapple, peach, cream cheese, salad, pasta salad, potato salad, chutney, pickle, gherkins, chicken or turkey, mayonnaise, coleslaw, asparagus

Pork – chutney, salad, coleslaw, apple, celery, mayonnaise, nuts, raisins, prunes

Bacon – scrambled egg, egg mayonnaise, avocado, chicken, lettuce and tomato, salad, potato salad, pasta salad, cream cheese, spinach, mushroom, sweetcorn, mayonnaise, hard cheese, peanut butter

Sausage – mustard, chutney, mayonnaise, salad, pasta salad, potato salad, coleslaw, scrambled egg, cheese

Scrambled eggs – bacon, smoked salmon, ham, sausage

Egg mayonnaise – bacon, ham, spinach, mushroom, sweetcorn, mustard and cress, spring onion, salad, potato salad, smoked salmon, shrimps, lumpfish roe, watercress

Tuna – spring onion, apple, cucumber, salad, pasta salad, potato salad, sweetcorn, hard cheese, peppers, anchovies, olives, coleslaw, cucumber, mayonnaise

Shrimps/Prawns – mayonnaise, cucumber, salad, pasta salad, avocado

Cream cheese – ham, bacon, peach, cucumber, raisins, dates, walnuts, grated hard cheese, salad, apple, pineapple, chives, red pepper, olives, coleslaw, watercress, mustard and cress

Hard Cheese – chutney, pickle, ham, bacon, tuna, pineapple, walnuts, raisins, apple, dates, tomato, salad, pasta salad, sweetcorn, mayonnaise, olives, gherkins, mustard and cress

Bananas – strawberry jam, honey, walnuts, dates

Peanut butter – bacon, jam, honey, chicken/turkey

◩ WALNUT & RAISIN BREAD ◪

½pt (300ml) water
¼pt (150ml) milk
½oz (15g) fat
pinch sugar
½oz (15g) fresh yeast (or
  equivalent dried)

12oz (350g) wholemeal flour
12oz (350g) plain white flour
1 teaspoon salt
3oz (75g) walnuts
3oz (75g) raisins

Put water, milk and fat into a saucepan and heat gently until fat is melted. Take off heat and add sugar, then sprinkle yeast over the warm liquid and mix gently. Sieve and mix the flours in a large bowl and make a well in the middle. Pour in the liquid and the salt and mix well. Knead for at least ten minutes until the dough is shiny and elastic. Cover the bowl with a damp cloth and leave to rise in a warm place for an hour or more, until doubled in size.

K nead again thoroughly, cover and leave to rise again for 45 minutes. Knead again, break walnuts into pieces and push dough out into a rectangle. Sprinkle half the raisins and nuts on to the dough, then fold one third in, then the other fold on top, like folding a letter in three. Turn the dough and push out into a rectangle the other way. Sprinkle remaining nuts and raisins and fold up again. Form into a ball and place on greased baking tray. Flatten the top a little, cut a cross and sprinkle the top with plain flour. Cover with dry cloth and leave to prove in a warm place until doubled in size. Preheat oven to 425°F, 220°C, gas mark 7. Bake for 30 to 40 minutes. The loaf is ready if it sounds hollow when tapped on the bottom.

This bread is very good for sandwiches, especially cheese.

◩ SPANISH TORTILLA ◪

6 PEOPLE

An authentic Spanish recipe from Concha Perez, who has kindly let us reproduce it. She stresses that the secret of this recipe is to use plenty of olive oil. For colour, use a red pepper. First blacken it all over under the grill, then peel, de-seed, slice thinly and add to the egg mixture.

2¼lb (1kg) potatoes
½pt (250ml) olive oil
8 eggs

chopped parsley if available
salt and pepper
1 Spanish onion, chopped

Peel potatoes and slice very thinly. Heat oil in a frying pan and when hot, fry potatoes, but do not allow to brown. Beat eggs in a large bowl, add finely chopped parsley and season with salt and pepper. Chop onions finely and add to frying pan, dribbling in more oil if necessary. When potatoes and onions are cooked but not browned, remove from the pan, leaving behind oil, and add to egg mixture.

Make sure you have about 2 tablespoons (30ml) of hot oil in the frying pan, either taking away the excess and keeping it in a cup, or adding to make up to this amount. Pour in the egg mixture and cook over a moderate heat, shaking constantly to avoid sticking. After five or so minutes, place a large plate over the frying pan and invert omelette on to plate so golden crust is on top. Scrape any crusty bits from pan, add another 2 tablespoons of oil and slide the tortilla back into the frying pan, moist side down. Continue to cook, shaking for about 5 minutes or until bottom is golden brown, then turn on to a plate. To serve, cut in wedges like a cake.

◩ FRITTATAS ◪
with Tomato, Basil & Cheese

6 PEOPLE

Unlike tortillas, frittatas are thin pancake omelettes and should be taken in a stack to the picnic. They can be served flat, or rolled up and eaten with fingers.

1 medium Spanish onion
2 tablespoons chopped fresh basil
4 tomatoes
olive oil
6 eggs

2 tablespoons (30ml) milk
2oz (50g) grated parmesan
salt and pepper
butter

Finely chop onion and basil. Pour boiling water over tomatoes, leave two minutes, then rinse under cold water. Peel, cut in quarters and discard pips. Chop remaining flesh finely. Heat 2 tablespoons (30ml) olive oil in a frying pan and sauté onion until soft, then add tomatoes and basil for a few minutes. Beat eggs in bowl, add milk, grated cheese and tomato mixture. Season to taste. In small frying pan, heat butter until bubbling, then pour in a ladleful of mixture, enough for a thin pancake. Turn down heat and cook gently until firm, then flip over for a few minutes before taking out. Stir mixture between taking ladles out to cook. When cold, stack frittatas like pancakes.

An alternative filling is courgette and onion. Follow instructions as above, substituting 2 thinly sliced, medium courgettes for the tomato and basil. The courgettes will need to be cooked for as long as the onions.

◧ PASTIES ◨

6 PEOPLE

1 onion	*1lb (450g) mince beef*
1 carrot	*3oz (75g) butter*
1 parsnip	*chutney*
1 large potato	*beaten egg yolk to glaze*
1½lb (675g) shortcrust pastry	

Preheat oven to 400°F, 200°C, gas mark 6. Peel and chop vegetables finely, keeping them separate. Divide all ingredients including pastry into six portions. Take one portion of pastry and roll out into a round about ¼in (½cm) thick. Spread one portion of the potato in the centre of the pastry, then layer a portion of the meat, onion, carrot and parsnip on top of that. Season well with salt and pepper and add a knob of butter and a teaspoonful of chutney. Fold the pastry up and pinch the edges together to make a good seal, leaving a small hole at the top of the pasty to let the steam escape. Brush with beaten egg yolk and place on a greased baking sheet. Repeat with the other five pasties and bake near the top of the oven for 10 minutes, then reduce to 350°F, 180°C, gas mark 4 for 30 minutes. The pasty should be golden brown and will keep warm for some time if wrapped in foil, then a tea-towel and insulated with newspaper.

◩ SAUSAGE & CHEESE ROLLS ◪

6 PEOPLE

8oz (225g) packet frozen puff
  pastry
1 onion
1 tablespoon (15ml) oil
2 good teaspoons (10ml) mustard

6oz (175g) hard cheese
1lb (450g) sausagemeat
4oz (125g) stuffing mix (sage &
  onion or your favourite)
milk for glazing

Preheat oven to 450°F, 230°C, gas mark 8. Thaw and divide pastry into two. Peel and chop onion finely and sauté in oil until soft and turning golden. Roll out each pastry half thinly into a rectangle and spread the mustard down the middle of each. Grate cheese and mix together with onion, sausagemeat and stuffing mix. Form into two rolls and place on top of the mustard. Roll up sides to meet in the middle and secure join, or if preferred, cut pastry on each side to form diagonal strips, brush with milk and fold over filling to make a plait. Brush top with milk, place on baking trays and cook for 30 to 40 minutes or until cooked through and golden. Cool thoroughly and serve sliced.

An alternative to the stuffing mix is to add three tablespoons of your favourite chutney to the mixture.

◩ SCOTCH EGGS ◪

6 PEOPLE

6 hard-boiled eggs
1 tablespoon Dijon mustard
12oz (350g) breadcrumbs

12oz (350g) sausagemeat
2 eggs

Beat the raw eggs and mustard together in a shallow bowl and place half the breadcrumbs in another. Divide the sausagemeat into six and coat an egg completely with one portion. Dip it in the egg and mustard mixture and then into the breadcrumbs so it is evenly covered all over. Repeat with two more eggs, then add the rest of the breadcrumbs to the bowl and repeat with the last three. Chill the eggs in the fridge for at least three hours. Heat 3in (7.5cm) of oil in a pan or deep fat fryer and when sizzling hot, fry the eggs, not too many at a time, turning once or twice, for 10–15 minutes or until well browned. Leave to drain and cool completely on kitchen towel. Take a mustard or chutney to dip the eggs into.

For children or for smart picnics, quails' eggs can be used for delicate, bite-sized morsels.

For vegetarians or for a change or choice, substitute grated cheddar cheese for sausagemeat and serve with a fruit chutney.

◩ CHICKEN LEGS IN BACON ◪

6 PEOPLE

6 chicken drumsticks	6 rashers streaky bacon
salt and pepper	thyme

Preheat oven to 350°F, 180°C, gas mark 4. Season drumsticks with salt and pepper, and thyme. Cut off bacon rinds and wrap each drumstick in a rasher of bacon, securing with a cocktail stick if necessary. Put in baking tray and cook for 20–30 minutes or until bacon is crispy and chicken cooked through, turning at least once. Allow to cool completely before packing.

◩ PANFORTE ◪

6 PEOPLE

This recipe, given to us by Simone Sekers, will make two 7in panfortes. They keep very well for at least a month so it is worth making two, which will feed more than six, rather than halving the quantities for six. Panforte is a solid disc about $\frac{1}{2}$–$\frac{3}{4}$in (1.25–1.75cm) in depth. Try to avoid using ready chopped candied peel – a good delicatessen or supermarket should supply whole candied peel. Err slightly on the side of generosity when weighing the honey as it is better to have a softer, stickier panforte than a rock-hard toothbreaker!

4oz (125g) blanched almonds	4oz (125g) plain flour
4oz (125g) skinned hazelnuts	2 teaspoons ground cinnamon
4oz (125g) candied orange peel	$\frac{1}{2}$ teaspoon ground allspice
4oz (125g) candied lemon peel	pinch ground cloves
2oz (50g) naturally coloured	4oz (125g) sugar
glacé cherries	4oz (125g) dark runny honey
1oz (25g) angelica	icing sugar
1oz (25g) candied apricots or	rice paper (optional)
crystallised pineapple	

Preheat oven to 275°F, 140°C, gas mark 1. Line two 7in (19cm) flan dishes with non-stick baking paper, then with rice paper if required. Spread nuts on a baking sheet and toast under the grill, turning frequently. Cool and chop roughly. Chop the fruit small, using sharp kitchen scissors, dipped frequently in boiling water to stop sticky build-up. Mix flour, nuts, fruits and spices together. Slowly heat the sugar and honey in a heavy pan until the sugar has dissolved. Bring to boiling point and, as it rises in the pan, remove from heat and pour over fruit and flour mixture, mixing immediately. It is heavy work but important to mix well so there are no pockets of flour left. Spoon the mixture into the prepared tins and smooth the tops with a spoon dipped in very hot water. Cook in oven for 45 minutes, then ease out of tins and leave to cool on a rack, before dusting copiously with icing sugar sifted with a pinch of cinnamon. Leave to set in cool, dry place for 24 hours, then wrap decoratively.

FAMILY PICNICS

FAMILY PICNICS

At Killerton in Devon, the Acland family had an unusual site for their picnics – the Bear's Hut in the garden. It was built in 1808 by the gardener John Veitch for the 10th Baronet, Sir Thomas Acland, as a surprise for his bride, Lydia, on her return from their honeymoon. It was intended to be a rustic hut, with a ceiling of matting and pine cones, a floor made from deers' knucklebones, but with the added unrural sophistications of a fireplace and stained-glass windows. Here the tea things were laid ever at the ready for the ladies of the house, or the children, to enjoy their picnics. At the end of the century, the hut, originally called Lady Cot, received its present name when it became home to a black bear, brought from Canada by the 14th Baronet. When not residing in his hut, this naughty bear was known to storm tea-shops in Cambridge in search of buns.

Family picnics were also a feature of Standen in West Sussex. The house was designed by Philip Webb and built between 1892 and 1894 for James Beale, a successful London solicitor. James and his wife Margaret wanted a roomy house for their large family of four girls and three boys, which grew ever larger with the arrival of their nineteen grandchildren. Four of these grandchildren, who became particularly devoted to Standen because they spent so many of their holidays there, put together their family memories. This is a description of picnics taken at Standen during the early years of this century:

> Picnic teas were often taken down to the rocky bank, with the pony cart to carry the provisions and the very young, driven by our nurse Nancy. The same pony, in great leather over-shoes, pulled the lawn mower in the garden. Each rock had its name (Castle, Tea Table, Cave, etc.), and the whole steep bank was a splendid adventure playground for all ages ...
>
> Each summer there was always a long drive to Cobnor ... on Chichester Harbour. We were all packed into the old Rolls, with great food hampers on the back. Though the long, rolling drives were sick-making, especially for those on the side-facing, tip-up seats, the huge lunch picnic on the Downs was much enjoyed. The chauffeur always removed the front passenger seat from the car for Grandmother to sit on, on the grassy slope.

◼ TOMATO, CARROT & ORANGE SOUP ◾

6 PEOPLE

Delicious hot or cold, this recipe can be served according to the weather, and for a change, you can substitute cider for the orange juice.

10oz (275g) onions
10oz (275g) carrots
3 tablespoons (45ml) olive oil or
  butter
salt and pepper

large tin (780g) tomatoes
¼pt (150ml) stock
¼pt (150ml) orange juice
cream and chopped chives to
  garnish (optional)

Peel and roughly chop onions and carrots. Sauté in the oil in a saucepan until onions are soft, but do not allow to brown. Season with salt and pepper, add the tin of tomatoes and stock and simmer gently until the carrots are soft. Blend until smooth and add orange juice. Check seasoning and either reheat to boiling point or chill before putting in thermos. Swirl with cream and/or sprinkle chives over each serving.

◼ CHEESE & ONION BREAD ◾

6 PEOPLE

This bread is delicious buttered with steaming bowls of soup. If made on the day, wrap it in foil and newspapers when it comes out of the oven to keep it hot.

½oz (15g) fresh yeast (or
  equivalent dried)
½pt (300ml) warm water
1lb (450g) plain white flour
1 teaspoon salt
3oz (75g) lard

1 large onion
1 tablespoon (15ml) oil
4oz (125g) cheddar
2 teaspoons mixed herbs
beaten egg to glaze (optional)

Preheat oven to 425°F, 220°C, gas mark 7. Dissolve the yeast in a little of the warm water. Sieve flour and salt into a bowl and make a well in the middle. Pour yeast into the well, add 1oz (25g) lard, flaked and then the rest of the water. Mix together and knead well for 5–10 minutes. Cover with a damp cloth and leave in a warm place to rise for 1 hour. Peel and finely chop onion and sauté until soft and golden in the oil. Roll the dough out into a ½in (1.25cm) thick rectangular shape. Flake half the remaining lard, grate one half of the cheese and sprinkle half the herbs and onions evenly over the rectangle. Fold dough into three like folding a letter and seal the edges. Leave covered in the fridge for 15 minutes. Roll into a rectangle again and sprinkle remaining onion, flaked lard, herbs and grated cheese over it. Fold into three, seal edges and leave in fridge for 15 minutes. Take out and press into a greased loaf tin or deep round cake tin. Score the top diagonally with a knife to make diamond shapes and leave to rise in a warm place until doubled. Brush top with beaten egg and bake for 30–40 minutes.

Try alternative fillings or additions to the cheese, herbs and onions. Chopped olives, ham and sun-dried tomatoes are all delicious.

◣ CHICKEN LIVER PÂTÉ ◢

6 PEOPLE

1 teaspoon green peppercorns (optional)
1 tablespoon (15ml) brandy or sherry
½ small onion

2oz (50g) butter
8oz (225g) chicken livers
2 tablespoons single cream (optional)

Crush peppercorns and soak in the brandy or sherry for about half an hour. Chop onion finely and sauté in butter. When translucent, add livers and seasoning and cook gently for about ten minutes. Blend until smooth, adding cream if a richer, smoother pâté is required, then add spirit and peppercorns and blend briefly. Turn into dish and chill.

◣ MIDDLE EASTERN MEATLOAF ◢
or Meatloaf with Chestnuts & Sultanas

6 PEOPLE

Serve this meatloaf with a dish that will double as a sauce for it, such as peperonata, ratatouille (the filling without the tart), tomato mould, tomato salad or carrot salad.

24 chestnuts (if using dried, soak for several hours)
vegetable or olive oil
1 large, or 2 small onions
4 slices brown or white bread for breadcrumbs
2 eggs

1½lb (675g) lean minced beef or lamb
4oz (125g) sultanas
good handful chopped parsley
2 teaspoons mixed spice (or 1 teaspoon allspice and pinch of cinnamon, ginger and nutmeg)
salt and freshly ground pepper

Preheat oven to 375°F, 190°C, gas mark 5. Rub chestnuts with oil and roast for 30 minutes or until golden brown, then chop roughly. Finely chop onion and make breadcrumbs (both can be put into processor until finely chopped). Beat the eggs and mix all ingredients together in a large bowl. Flatten into lined and greased baking dish or tin and bake for 1 hour. Do not overcook.

Walnuts can be used instead of chestnuts, and for a treat pine nuts can be substituted.

◪ WELL-FILLED QUICHE ◪

6 PEOPLE

There is nothing more delicious than a quiche so full of goodies you can't taste that there is any egg mixture in it, rather than the dull and colourless supermarket quiches which are all egg mixture and a little bit of bacon or onion somewhere! Below is the recipe for a well-filled quiche with alternative ingredients which can be added or substituted.

1 portion of pastry (see p.100)	3 eggs
6–8 slices streaky bacon	2¾ fl oz (75ml) milk
1 medium onion, chopped	4oz (125g) cheddar cheese
3 tomatoes, sliced	2¾ fl oz (75ml) single cream
7oz (200g) can sweetcorn	(optional)
(preferably with pimentoes)	

Preheat oven to 350°F, 180°C, gas mark 4. Lightly grease an 8in (20cm) flan dish, roll out the pastry and place in flan dish, pressing in gently all round. In a frying pan, gently cook bacon. Peel and finely chop onion and add to frying pan. Pour boiling water over tomatoes, leave for 3 minutes, then peel and slice. When onions are golden brown, spread them over the pastry base. Drain corn and pour over onion. Chop the bacon roughly when cooked and de-rind if necessary. Sprinkle evenly over the corn, then cover with tomato slices. Beat eggs and stir in milk, salt and pepper and cream. Grate and add half the cheese and pour this mixture over the dish. Grate the rest of the cheese on top and bake in the oven for 30 minutes or until it is set and golden brown.

Alternative ingredients that can be added: tuna fish; ham; courgettes (sauté until soft with onions); mushrooms (sauté for a few minutes in butter or oil); red or yellow pepper (chopped or sliced); leeks (sauté until soft); any fresh herbs you have in the garden (finely chopped); shrimps or prawns; olives.

◣ CHICKEN SALAD ◢

6 PEOPLE

1 chicken
1 medium onion, skinned and
   halved
salt and pepper
1 pinch mixed herbs
4oz (125g) seedless green grapes
4oz (125g) blanched almonds

1 large Granny Smith apple
curry powder
4 tablespoons mayonnaise
1 teaspoon (5ml) lemon juice
2oz (50g) sultanas or raisins
1 box cress
finely chopped fresh parsley

Put chicken in a pan with the halved onion, salt, pepper and mixed herbs. Barely cover with water, bring to the boil and simmer for 1 hour or until tender. Strain liquid and set aside for use as stock. Discard all skin and bone from the chicken and cut in neat bite-size pieces. Halve grapes, grill almonds gently until golden brown and split or chop roughly. De-core and chop apple. Mix a good pinch of curry powder with mayonnaise or more to taste. Add lemon juice and mix well, then add all other ingredients and toss well until all are coated. Sprinkle salad with parsley.

◣ MIXED SALADS ◢

With the numerous varieties of lettuce and herbs, and the abundance of salad ingredients now available in supermarkets, there is no excuse for a dull salad. Edible flowers can be used for decoration to make the salad look special as well as taste good.

Mixed salads can be made up of just about anything, and the make-up of the salad should depend on your personal taste and the ingredients you have in your fridge, larder and garden. For a colourful picnic display, separate ingredients to make different salads – green salad, tomato salad, bean salad, cucumber salad, potato salad, carrot-based salad. Recipes are included in this book for these salads, but for an easy picnic, make a one-dish salad with all your favourite ingredients in it.

For a picnic, chop each ingredient into bite-size pieces so the salad can be easily eaten with a fork. Trying to chop lettuce with a fork is a bore, and trying to fold it often leads to a faceful of salad as it all comes undone when you raise it to your mouth. Much easier to do the chopping at home!

Leaves for salads

Iceberg lettuce – crisp, crunchy leaves make an ideal base for salads.

Little Gem lettuce – compact with crisp heart and good flavour and very little waste.

Cos – long, tasty crisp lettuce with good flavour, but a fair amount of leaves wasted.

Lambs lettuce – delicious, but mild flavoured little leaves. Use by itself or with few other ingredients, otherwise it will be overwhelmed.

Chicory – faintly bitter taste, crisp leaves.

Radicchio – a variety of red chicory with a bitter taste and good strong colour.

Endive – easily grown salad leaf related to chicory with bitter flavour. Leaves can be very frilly and decorative as in 'curly endive' or Frisée varieties.

'Lollo' lettuce – crunchy, frilly leaves in green or red, good for mixed leaf salads.

Chinese leaves – almost white salad leaves, very little waste.

Spinach – young leaves have the best flavour for salads.

Rocket – hot, spicy almost nutty flavour. Use young leaves as they become bitter when they get older.

Salad herbs

Mustard and cress – seedlings give hot flavour to salads. Allowed to grow on in the garden, the leaves can be used but get hotter as they get older!

Basil – leaves have warm, spicy flavour with many varieties. Good in all salads but goes particularly well with tomatoes.

Mint – many varieties, use leaves in salads, particularly with potato, cucumber and in fruit salads.

Thyme – Lemon-scented thyme leaves give a wonderful fresh flavour to salads, look good in the garden and also work well in fruit salads.

Parsley – leaves are not only tasty, but extremely beneficial to health.

Dill – chop leaves finely into salads, particularly potato salad.

Chives – chopped leaves and florets of flowers have a mild onion flavour, particularly good in potato salad.

Borage – young leaves have cucumber flavour.

Coriander – aromatic flavour to leaves.

Fennel – aromatic, faintly aniseed flavour, use leaves sparingly.

Lemon balm – lemony flavoured leaves.

Marjoram/oregano – spicy, savoury-flavoured leaves.

Nasturtium – sharp peppery flavoured leaves.

Tarragon – leaves have warm, peppery, aniseed flavour.

Flowers

Nasturtiums

Calendula/Marigolds – sprinkle individual petals.

Pansies

Violets

Borage

Chives – break flowers up into florets.

Rosemary

It is more effective to use flowers of similar colours in each salad than a mishmash of colours.

Other salad ingredients

Most vegetables can be used in salads either raw or dropped in boiling water for several minutes, then refreshed under the cold tap. Never overcook vegetables to be used in salads; they should remain crisp.

Fruits are delicious and refreshing in salads, though avoid fruits which will go soft or discoloured. Oranges, grapes and apples (dipped in lemon juice and added a short time before eating) are particularly good. Try dried fruit such as currants and dates.

Sprouting seeds are not only delicious in salads, but particularly nourishing. Try bean sprouts, mustard and cress, alfalfa and mung bean sprouts.

Nuts, roasted or not, add a different flavour and texture to salads, but do not leave dressed for too long – better to add them at the picnic.

The same advice goes for croûtons, which again add flavour and a crunchy texture. To make croûtons, brush both sides of bread slices with oil and bake until crisp and golden. Flavouring such as herbs, crushed garlic or celery salt can be added to the oil if required.

Cheese and/or meats can also be added to salads to make a meal in one bowl. Dice, grate or cut into matchsticks as required.

Decorative salads

Instead of mixing salads as normal, a wonderful display can be achieved by using a flat bowl or dish and separating the ingredients. Chop roughly or grate selected ingredients and arrange in lines across the dish, in rings or in sections as in cake slices, to make a colourful display. Choose from the following ingredients or select your own: chopped avocado; chopped chicken; chopped tomato; grated cheddar; grated carrots; flaked crabmeat; finely chopped egg, with white and yolk separated; chopped cucumber; chopped watercress; chopped green or red pepper.

◣ CLAIRE'S VINAIGRETTE ◢

$\frac{1}{4}$ or $\frac{1}{2}$ clove garlic (depending on personal taste)
2 teaspoons Dijon mustard
1 tablespoon (15ml) sugar

2 tablespoons (30ml) white wine vinegar
black pepper and salt
6 tablespoons (90ml) olive oil

Crush garlic into a bowl and mix all ingredients, except oil, together well. Slowly dribble in oil, mixing all the time. The mixture will thicken and is ready at this point. If there is oil remaining when it thickens, taste and add oil only if the mixture is too sharp.

◣ MUSHROOM VINAIGRETTE ◢

6 PEOPLE

1 onion
4 tablespoons (60ml) oil
2 courgettes
2 tomatoes

9oz (250g) mushrooms
salt and pepper
vinaigrette (see above)
parsley, chopped

Sauté onion in 2 tablespoons of oil until translucent. Turn into serving bowl. Add another 2 tablespoons of oil and slice and sauté courgettes for a few minutes. Meanwhile, pour boiling water over tomatoes, leave to soak for a minute, then peel. Wash or peel mushrooms and chop these and the tomatoes and add to the courgettes, turning frequently to cook all over. Do not overcook as the vegetables should not be soft. Add to the onions, season with salt and pepper and leave to cool. Not too long before the picnic, toss the vegetables in vinaigrette and decorate with fresh chopped parsley.

If you wish to add other vegetables, broccoli, green beans, cauliflower, carrots and celery can all be used as alternatives or additions.

◣ RICE SALAD ◢

6 PEOPLE

This recipe, provided by my mother, is a standard and highly popular feature at Crookenden family picnics. It seems most people expect a bland, 90 per cent rice salad when this dish is announced, whereas it is full of goodies and will certainly be in heavy demand.

9oz (250g) long grain rice
3 tablespoons (45ml) vinaigrette
  (see p.44)
salt and pepper
1 teaspoon curry powder
2oz (50g) almonds
1 onion, finely chopped
2 sticks celery

1 cooking apple
2 tablespoons (30ml) lemon juice
4oz (125g) frozen peas
6oz (175g) cooked ham
6oz (175g) cooked chicken
2 small tins shrimps or ½pt
  (300ml) fresh prawns
2 tablespoons chopped parsley

Cook the rice in boiling water until just done. Rinse under hot water, then cold and drain until dry. When still warm, put into serving bowl and mix in vinaigrette, adding salt and pepper to taste. Mix in curry powder. Toast almonds under grill on medium heat, turning until brown and allow to cool before adding. Shred or chop onion and celery very finely, peel and chop cooking apple, dip in lemon juice and add to bowl. Drop peas into boiling water and simmer for 2 minutes. Run under cold tap, then drain and add. Chop ham and chicken, drain shrimps and add to bowl with parsley, mixing together well. Add lemon juice to taste. Leave to cool in fridge for at least an hour.

If you are preparing this dish the day before or well in advance, keep the almonds to one side and add before packing the dish for the picnic to keep them from going soft.

If preferred, a mixture of mayonnaise and vinaigrette can be added to the rice instead of just vinaigrette.

◣ CARROT SALAD ◢

6 PEOPLE

1½lb (675g) carrots
1 green pepper
1 medium onion
1 10oz (300g) tin tomato soup

1 tablespoon sugar
1 tablespoon (15ml) oil
1 tablespoon (15ml) vinegar
salt and pepper

Peel and cut carrots in rings, halved if too large, then simmer in water until cooked. De-seed and slice pepper and onion into matchsticks and cook in tomato soup, sugar, oil and vinegar until vegetables are soft. Mix in carrots, season with salt and pepper, and cool. If possible, leave overnight in the fridge.

◣ EASY TOMATO MOULD ◪

6 PEOPLE

15oz (435g) can Heinz tomato
soup
7oz (200g) cream cheese
1 packet gelatine
4fl oz (100ml) hot water
4oz (125g) mayonnaise
2–3oz (50–75g) celery very
finely sliced

2–3oz (50–75g) spring onions
finely chopped
½ teaspoon (2.5ml)
Worcestershire sauce
pinch of cayenne pepper
¼ teaspoon sugar
¼ teaspoon salt

Heat soup and cheese over low heat, whisking until smooth. Dissolve gelatine in the water. Pour soup mixture over gelatine and mix well. When cool, add mayonnaise and other ingredients. Pour into a moistened mould. Refrigerate for several hours to set.

Should the mixture not be solid enough after several hours, pour into saucepan and gently warm. Meanwhile dissolve ½ packet of gelatine in a little hot water, add to warm mixture and stir well. Pour back into clean and moistened mould and refrigerate to set.

◣ PASTRY FOR FRUIT TARTS ◪

6 PEOPLE

6oz (180g) soft butter
8oz (225g) plain flour
1 tablespoon icing sugar

1 egg yolk
iced water

Preheat oven to 450°F, 230°C, gas mark 8. Dice butter and sieve flour and icing sugar. Mix gently together with fingers until the mixture resembles fine crumble. Mix the egg yolk with an equal amount of iced water and add to the pastry. Mix dough with spoon until well blended. Roll into ball, wrap in towel and leave in fridge for 30 minutes. When ready, roll out on floured surface, turning every so often, mending splits by pressing together with fingers. Roll pastry gently over rolling pin and press loosely into tin. Cut off any excess.

Prick pastry all over with a fork, line with foil or waxed paper and cover with dried beans to stop pastry rising. (Beans can be kept in a jar for this purpose and used again and again.) Bake for 10–15 minutes in a hot oven, but do not let pastry brown. Then remove beans and foil and cook for another 10–15 minutes at 350°F, 180°C, gas mark 4. Again, pastry should not pass golden brown.

It is easier to use a pastry tin with a loose bottom so that the ring can be removed when the tart is finished, and the tart transported on the metal bottom. This looks good, but is firmly supported underneath.

When the pastry has completely cooled, fill with a layer of whipped cream and then pile on the fruit of your choice and dust with sugar. Berries should be arranged with the stalk end down in the cream in a spiral from the centre. If strawberries are too big, chop in half and arrange cut side down. Peaches should be sliced and spiralled overlapping each slice. For a colourful effect, mix fruits with, say, sliced peaches around the outside, then strawberries, then blueberries in the centre or whichever fruits are available at the time. If required, the fruit can be glazed by melting the same flavour jam or jelly with a little water and, as it cools, pouring it over the fruit.

◥ SUMMER PUDDING ◢

6 PEOPLE

There are many recipes for summer pudding, as it is a classic and ideal for picnics. To avoid accidents, keep in the pudding bowl and turn out at picnic, not before!

Any combination of fruits is delicious, but it is wise to cook lightly blueberries and red-, black- or whitecurrants beforehand. If you are using only raspberries, strawberries and blackberries, it is a good idea to cook say 4oz (125g) to ensure there is enough juice for the bread to soak up. Clean currants or berries and let them steep in a small pan sprinkled with sugar and 1 tablespoon (15ml) lemon juice. Cook with no extra liquid for a few minutes over a gentle heat.

half a large loaf of two-day-old
  white bread
2½lb (1125g) raspberries,
  redcurrants, strawberries,
  blackberries, whitecurrants,
  blackcurrants or blueberries

2 tablespoons (30ml) lemon juice
3oz (75g) caster sugar

Remove crusts from bread and slice thinly. Line a deep pudding bowl with bread slices, keeping back some for the lid. Keep lining even, using a dab of butter where necessary to keep bread in shape. Mix the fruit with lemon juice and sugar and fill bread shell. Top with bread slices to form lid. Rest a plate or saucer on the lid and weigh down. Leave in fridge for 8 hours, preferably overnight. At picnic, place serving plate over the pudding bowl and invert. Gently unmould, decorate with fresh fruit or mint leaves and serve with cream.

If you wish, extra fruit can be cooked and puréed and taken to the picnic to serve as a sauce with the pudding and cream.

◣ CHOCOLATE POTS ◿

6 PEOPLE

Do remember that all foods with raw eggs should be kept chilled until eaten, so give this priority in the coolbox or pack with ice and insulate well with newspapers.

6oz (175g) plain chocolate   *3 eggs, separated*
2 tablespoons (30ml) water   *$\frac{1}{4}$pt (150ml) double cream*
$\frac{1}{2}$oz (15g) butter

Melt chocolate with the water, over a pan of simmering water. Stir from time to time and when melted and smooth, remove from heat. Stir in butter and beat in egg yolks one at a time. Whisk egg whites until stiff, and when the chocolate mixture is cool, fold in the whites. Mix thoroughly, then pour into ramekins. Chill, preferably overnight and keep cold until eaten.

Alternatives to this recipe you can try:

Alcoholic chocolate pots – add 1 tablespoon (15ml) rum or brandy with the butter

Mocha pots – add 2 teaspoons (10ml) instant coffee or camp coffee to the 2 tablespoons of water which should be boiling hot before melting chocolate. A tablespoon (15ml) of Kahlua can be added with the butter if required.

Orange and chocolate pots – melt chocolate in 2 tablespoons (30ml) orange juice instead of water. Add finely grated rind of $\frac{1}{2}$ orange with the butter. A tablespoon (15ml) of Grand Marnier can be added with the butter if required.

CHILDREN'S
PICNICS

CHILDREN'S PICNICS

E very year, on the day after school broke up for the holidays, a children's tea-party was held at the great Neo-classical mansion at Ickworth in Suffolk, given by the Marquess and Marchioness of Bristol. This description, dating from the early years of this century, comes from Zoë Ward's *Courtsy to the Lady*:

> We had heard of the school treat as soon as we entered the Infants' School, and long before the time came for us to attend we knew every rule and taboo, everything that was expected of us on that greatest of days. And just to make sure that we did, just before we broke up for the summer holidays on a fine July Friday afternoon, we were given a talk ... on how we were to behave at the party.
>
> My excitement was somewhat dampened when I found that the only person with time on her hands was my headmistress grandmother, whose school in Lincolnshire must have broken up the day before we did. Anyway, she was better than nobody, so I poured out to her all the instructions we had been given ... how we were to take our mugs, to be under the beech tree on the Green at three o'clock, to be clean and tidy, to speak quietly, to keep with our partners – mine being Barbara Collins, who knew even more about the Bristols than I did, her father being their butler – not to get out of line, and not to walk in the cowpats, of which there were plenty in the park, and so on and so forth.
>
> 'We go along Geraldine's Walk,' I said 'and Lord and Lady Bristol will be waiting for us on the lawn, and we all go up to them, and say "good afternoon", and the boys bow, and the girls curtsy ...'
>
> I was not prepared for the explosion caused by that simple remark. My grandmother swelled to twice her normal size, her usually pale face turned purple, and she hissed, 'You will do no such thing! No grandchild of mine shall curtsy to anybody. You are as good as they are – and if I hear you have curtsied – I'll floor you!' (That was a favourite threat of hers.)

The author, who took instant refuge in the pig sty, had not realised that while the estate around Ickworth was still strongly feudal in its outlook, her grandmother had spent years away and had rejected this attitude. She played for time by getting to the back of the crocodile, waiting to greet the Bristols. In the event, there were too many children to be presented and they were merely asked to say 'Good Afternoon'. Having duly bellowed their greetings, they broke ranks and raced to the food:

Long tables were set up under the trees, and the staff were busy setting out the tea – mountains of bread and butter, slices of fruit cake, and plates of iced Genoese sponge, cut into small pieces. The latter were very popular and much sought after; needless to say, we little ones never had a piece!

◤ PICK & MIX ◢

Cut any combination of the following into bite-sized pieces and either thread on to skewers or pack into individual lunch boxes. Do not let children run around with skewers which are sharp and can be dangerous.

Sandwiches – any fillings, sweet
  or savoury
Chicken
Ham
Pineapple
Sausages
Salami/spicy sausage
Firm meatballs
Carrot slices
Mangetout
Mushrooms
Cauliflower
Olives
Cheese

Pickles
Cold new potatoes
Cherry tomatoes
Cucumber
Raisins
Peaches
Strawberries
Plums
Grapes
Raw jelly cubes
Brownies
Slices of Mars bars or other
  chocolate
Marshmallows

◤ PORCUPICK ◢

6 PEOPLE

1 tablespoon mango or other fruit
  chutney
9oz (250g) cream cheese or
  drained cottage cheese
4oz (125g) cheddar, finely grated
currants for decoration

raw vegetables such as carrots,
celery, courgettes, cucumber,
red or yellow peppers, peeled
where necessary and cut into
matchsticks
biscuit crackers

Chop up any lumps of fruit in the chutney, then combine with the cheeses, adding a little milk if necessary to achieve an adhesive consistency. Reserve a little of the mixture to make a small head; with lightly floured hands, shape the remaining mixture into a ball and place on a serving dish. With reserved mixture, make a head using currants for eyes and nose. At the picnic, stick the matchsticks of vegetables into the ball of cheese to make the porcupick. Take crackers to use when the vegetables have been finished.

◪ MINI PIZZAS ◪

6 PEOPLE

½oz (15g) fresh yeast (or
   equivalent in dried)
1 teaspoon sugar
¼pt (150ml) warm water
10oz (275g) plain white flour
1 teaspoon salt
5 tablespoons (75ml) oil
1 onion
1 clove garlic
2 tablespoons (30ml) oil

2 tablespoons tomato purée
14oz (400g) tin tomatoes
1 tablespoon basil, marjoram or
   oregano or a mixture
salt and pepper
8oz (225g) mushrooms
4oz (125g) cheddar or mozzarella
4oz (125g) spicy sausage (salami,
   pepperoni, etc.)
good pinch of sugar

Dissolve yeast and sugar in warm water and leave to stand and ferment for 10 minutes. Meanwhile, sieve flour and salt into a bowl and make a well in the centre. Pour in the yeast mixture and oil and mix well. Knead for a good five minutes to a soft dough. Cover and leave to rise for an hour.

Meanwhile line two baking trays with baking parchment or oil and lightly flour. Chop onion and crush garlic and sauté in 2 tablespoons of oil until translucent. Add tomato pureé, tin of tomatoes, breaking up the tomatoes to a pulp, herbs and seasonings. Simmer gently until reduced to a thick coating sauce. Peel or wash and chop mushrooms and sauté in 1 tablespoon oil until cooked. Grate cheese and slice sausage. Bring out dough and knead again. Take a small handful of dough, place on a floured board and flatten gently. Pick it up by an edge and move your hands around the outside, letting it stretch by its own weight to a small circle – be careful it does not tear. Lay this on the baking sheet and repeat until dough is finished. Spread tomato sauce over the pizza bases, top with mushrooms and sliced sausage and finally the cheese.

Preheat oven to 425°F, 220°C, gas mark 7. Leave pizzas in a warm place to prove for 30 minutes, then bake at the bottom of the oven for about 30 minutes or until base is golden and cooked through. Allow to cool completely before packing.

Alternative toppings: ham; minced beef; crispy bacon; chopped-up chicken; tuna; prawn; anchovy; olives; capers; sweetcorn; green or red peppers; chillies; and pineapple. Any combination of toppings can be used, but meats should be cooked first, either by themselves or in the tomato sauce.

◣ SAUSAGES ◢

For children, use cocktail or thin chipolata sausages. Adults also love sausages and they are always popular on a picnic. Here are some variations to try.

To cook sausages, preheat oven to 350°F, 180°C, gas mark 4 and bake for 15–20 minutes, turning once, until evenly browned.

Honey and herb sausages

Sausages are delicious, though sticky when cooked in honey and thyme, sage or rosemary. Put sausages in a roasting tin, sprinkle with chosen herb and drizzle honey over. Bake until well browned, shaking from time to time. Alternatively, roll the sausages in seed mustard or a fruit chutney before cooking to add flavour.

Cheesy sausages

Spread the sausages out in a roasting tin. Bake until browned, then remove from oven and allow to cool a little. Meanwhile, cut pieces of cheddar half the length and width of the sausages. Make a slit in each sausage but do not go right through the sausage. Insert the cheese well so it will not run out of the sausage when melted and put back into the oven until cheese is bubbling and beginning to brown. Leave to cool before packing, or wrap with foil, insulate with newspapers and pack in hot box.

Sausage and mash

Make buttery, not too solid mashed potato and mix with finely chopped raw spring onions or gently fried, finely chopped onion. Cook sausages until well browned, slit open and fill with mashed potato. Leave to cool before packing, or wrap with foil, insulate with newspapers and pack in hot box.

◨ SPAG & PORKY PIES ◪

6 PEOPLE

4oz (125g) plain flour
salt and pepper
cayenne pepper
2oz (50g) butter or margarine
2oz (50g) cheddar cheese

1 egg yolk
1 teaspoon (5ml) water
small can spaghetti hoops
2 Frankfurter sausages, chopped
1 egg

Preheat oven to 400°F, 200°C, gas mark 6. Sift together flour, pinch of salt and pinch of cayenne. Rub in the fat until the mixture resembles fine breadcrumbs. Grate cheese and add half to the mixture. Blend egg yolk and water and add to the mixture, mixing to a firm dough. Roll out pastry and line individual patty tins. Mix the spaghetti with chopped Frankfurters and remaining cheese and season to taste. Spoon into pastry cases and cut out lids to cover, sealing the edges with a little milk. Brush with beaten egg and bake for 15–20 minutes.

Try this recipe substituting chopped sausages and baked beans for the Frankfurters and spaghetti.

◨ FILLED MINI PITTA ◪

In most supermarkets you can now buy mini round pitta breads. These are very useful for children's picnics as they can be stuffed with filling, providing nourishment and taste without great wedges of bread. Coleslaw and salad will be eaten willingly in pitta as no knife and fork are required! Butter is not necessary with the fillings suggested below as they are all moist without it. To fill the pittas, lie them flat and with a knife slit open a third of the way round. Stand up, open out gently and fill.

Tuna fish, apple, lettuce and mayonnaise – mix together in a bowl the drained, flaked tuna, chopped apple and mayonnaise. Season to taste. Line the pitta with lettuce pieces and stuff with filling.

Coleslaw with Frankfurter, sausage or chicken – make coleslaw as in recipe on p.69. Add chopped sausage, Frankfurter or chicken as required and stuff into pitta.

Egg mayonnaise with mustard and cress – hard-boil eggs and run under cold tap to cool. Chop finely and mix with mayonnaise, salt and pepper. Put a pinch of mustard and cress in the pitta and fill with the egg mixture.

Cottage cheese with ham and peach – chop ham finely, peel and chop peach or nectarine and mix with cottage cheese. Stuff into pitta.

Bacon, cheese, lettuce and tomato – streaky bacon is best as it crisps well. Grill bacon until crisp, grate cheddar cheese, shred a crunchy lettuce such as iceberg finely and chop tomato. Combine together and add mayonnaise. The ingredients can be taken in separate bowls to the picnic and each child can stuff their own pitta.

These are just a few suggestions. Most salad ingredients can be combined into a pitta stuffing with or without meat or fish. For an easy and nourishing picnic, take a combination of raw vegetables (chopped and sliced into matchsticks, diced or cut into small florets), crispy bacon bits, chicken pieces, mayonnaise, mini pittas and the recipe for Porcupick on p.52 and the children can make their own stuffed pittas or dip the raw vegetable sticks as they wish.

◩ SUMMER FRUIT JELLY ◪

6 PEOPLE

This is a very good way of transporting and serving soft fruits for a children's picnic.

jelly cubes
8oz (225g) strawberries
8oz (225g) raspberries

2 peaches or nectarines
whipped cream (optional)

Make jelly as per instructions on packet. While cooling, prepare fruit, de-stalking raspberries and strawberries and peeling and stoning peaches. Halve any large strawberries. The fruit can be put into individual dishes and mixed with the jelly just before it sets, or put in a large glass dish. Decorate with whipped cream. If using individual dishes, each child's initial can be written on their dish with piped cream.

◩ BOSTON BROWNIES ◪

6 PEOPLE

2oz (50g) plain chocolate
2½oz (65g) margarine or butter
6oz (175g) caster sugar
2½oz (65g) self-raising flour
pinch of salt

2 eggs
½ teaspoon (2.5ml) vanilla
  essence
2oz (50g) walnuts

Preheat oven to 350°F, 180°C, gas mark 4. Grease and flour 8in (20cm) shallow square tin. Melt chocolate and butter in bowl over hot water, then in sugar. Sieve flour and salt. Beat eggs and add vanilla. Chop walnuts. Add chocolate, eggs and walnuts to flour and beat until smooth. Pour into tin and bake for 35 minutes. Cool in tin, then turn out and cut when cold.

◣ GINGERBREAD ◢

ABOUT 20 SQUARES

4oz (125g) butter	*2 teaspoons ground ginger*
1 tablespoon golden syrup	*½ teaspoon bicarbonate of soda*
2 tablespoons black treacle	*¼ teaspoon salt*
9oz (250g) plain flour	*½ teaspoon cinnamon*
3oz (75g) muscovado (or dark	*1 egg*
brown) sugar	*¼pt (150ml) milk*

Preheat oven to 375°F, 190°C, gas mark 5. Grease and line a 7in (18cm) square cake tin. In a small saucepan, heat until melted the butter, syrup and treacle. Sieve all dry ingredients into a bowl, make a well in the centre and pour in melted mixture, mixing well. Beat egg and stir this and the milk carefully into the mixture. Turn into the prepared cake tin and cook for 45 minutes or until a warm skewer pushed into the centre comes out cleanly. Turn out and cool on a wire tray, then cut into squares.

If required, 4oz (125g) of preserved stem ginger, drained and chopped, can be added to the mixture with the milk. Alternatively 3oz (75g) raisins can be added with the milk.

Gingerbread is delicious just plain, but if preferred, it can be iced. Recommended icings are orange, lemon or ginger.

For orange or lemon, melt 1oz (25g) butter in a saucepan, add juice of one lemon *or* juice of half an orange and 4oz (125g) icing sugar. Mix well and bring to the boil. Boil for a few minutes, leave to cool slightly, then drizzle all over cake.

For ginger, heat 1oz (25g) butter, 1 tablespoon of ginger syrup from stem ginger jar and 1½oz (40g) muscovado (or dark brown) sugar until sugar has dissolved. Bring to boil and boil for a few minutes. Leave to cool slightly and drizzle all over cake.

◣ CHOCOLATE BISCUIT CAKE ◢

6 PEOPLE

½ packet plain biscuits (Rich Tea,
    Digestives, etc.)
4oz (125g) butter

2 tablespoons golden syrup
4 tablespoons chocolate powder

Put the biscuits into a plastic bag and break up gently with a rolling pin.
A blender tends to crush the biscuits to dust. Melt the butter and when
just melted, take off heat and stir in golden syrup and chocolate powder.
Leave to cool slightly, then pour on to biscuits in a bowl. The mixture
can either be pressed down to about 2in (5cm) thick in a serving dish
and cut into fingers, or laid out on greaseproof paper and rolled into a
big sausage shape and sliced at the picnic. Chill.

◣ LEMONADE ◢

3 lemons
9oz (250g) sugar

4pt (2.4l) boiling water
ice cubes

Halve lemons, squeeze juice and pound skins into large container or
jug. Add sugar and stir. Pour over boiling water and stir until sugar is
completely dissolved. Leave to cool, then add ice cubes, stir and pour
into thermos.

   If you take normal fizzy lemonade to the picnic, instead of making
your own, take along some blackcurrant drink to add to the lemonade
to make 'Kir' – a much more special drink than plain lemonade!

◣ GINGER BEER ◢

1 lemon
1lb (450g) sugar
1oz (25g) cream of tartar
1oz (25g) root ginger

8pt (4.5l) water
1oz (25g) fresh yeast or
    4 teaspoons dried yeast

Peel lemon and squeeze and strain juice into large bowl or bucket. Add
peel, sugar and cream of tartar. Peel ginger and bruise well, then add.
Pour over boiling water and stir well. When cooled to just tepid, add
yeast. Cover and leave at least overnight to ferment. Skim and pour
through sieve into screw-topped bottles. Leave two days before
drinking.

SPORTING PICNICS

SPORTING PICNICS

In the nineteenth century sporting picnics became the acme of fashion, from cricket teas to boating suppers. Charles Dickens in *Pickwick Papers*, published in 1836–7, poked gentle fun at another culinary institution, the shooting picnic.

Mr Pickwick, suffering from rheumatism, is propelled by Sam Weller to the picnic site in a wheelbarrow. Due to the shooting skills – or rather the lack of them – of Mr Tupman and Mr Winkle, he is badly in need of alcoholic solace by midday when the basket is unpacked:

'Weal pie,' said Mr Weller, soliloquising, as he arranged the eatables on the grass. 'Wery good thing is weal pie, when you know the lady as made it, and is quite sure it an't kittens . . . Tongue; well that's a wery good thing when it an't a woman's. Bread – knuckle o'ham, reg'lar picter – cold beef in slices, wery good. What's in them stone jars, young touch-and-go?'

'Beer in this one,' replied the boy, taking from his shoulder a couple of large stone bottles, fastened together by a leathern strap – 'cold punch in t'other.'

. . . 'Well that certainly is most capital cold punch,' said Mr Pickwick, looking earnestly at the stone bottle; 'and the day is extremely warm, and – Tupman, my dear friend, a glass of punch?'

'With the greatest delight,' replied Mr Tupman; and having drank that glass, Mr Pickwick took another, just to see whether there was any orange peel in the punch, because orange peel always disagreed with him; and finding that there was not, Mr Pickwick took another glass to the health of their absent friend, and then felt himself imperatively called upon to propose another in honour of the punch-compounder, unknown.

This constant succession of glasses produced considerable effect upon Mr Pickwick; his countenance beamed with the most sunny smiles, laughter played around his lips, and good-humoured merriment twinkled in his eye. Yielding by degrees to the influence of the exciting liquid, rendered more so by the heat, Mr Pickwick expressed a strong desire to recollect a song which he had heard in his infancy, and the attempt proving abortive, sought to stimulate his memory with more glasses of punch, which appeared to have quite a contrary effect; for, from forgetting the words of the song, he began to forget how to articulate any words at all; and finally, after rising to his legs to address the company in an eloquent speech, he fell into the barrow, and fast asleep, simultaneously.

◣ VICHYSSOISE ◢
Leek & Potato Soup
6 PEOPLE

4lb (1.8kg) leeks
1½lb (675g) potatoes
4oz (125g) butter
1½pt (900ml) chicken stock
salt and freshly ground black
  pepper

pinch finely grated or ground
  nutmeg
¼pt (150ml) single cream
chives to garnish

Trim and wash leeks and peel potatoes. Chop leeks roughly and sauté in butter in saucepan until soft but not brown. Slice potatoes and add to saucepan with stock, salt, pepper and nutmeg and simmer until vegetables are cooked. Blend until smooth, add a little more stock or water if the consistency is too thick. Stir in cream and adjust seasoning as necessary. Depending on the weather, this can be served hot or chilled – chill overnight or heat to boiling point before pouring into thermos. Take chopped chives to sprinkle on individual servings.

◣ FARMHOUSE PÂTÉ ◢

Very easy to make, this recipe will fill one of the round dishes in which pâté is sold in delicatessens. If any of this popular pâté is left over, it will keep well in the fridge.

2oz (50g) onions, chopped
1 dessertspoon (10ml) vegetable
  oil
8oz (225g) streaky bacon
8oz (225g) pig's liver
2 anchovy fillets
½ clove garlic

2 eggs
¼pt (150ml) cream
3oz (75g) breadcrumbs
salt and pepper
grated nutmeg
4 bay leaves

Preheat oven to 325°F, 160°C, gas mark 3. Gently fry onions in oil and remove rind from bacon. Blend liver, onions, anchovies, garlic and half the amount of bacon. Beat eggs with cream and add breadcrumbs. Mix into liver and add seasoning. Line a dish with 2 bay leaves and the remaining bacon. Pour in mixture and cover with bacon and 2 more bay leaves. Cover with foil and bake for 1½ hours or until cooked through.

◣ TARAMASALATA ◢

6 PEOPLE

3 slices of white bread
water
4oz (125g) smoked cod's roe
½ small onion

4 or 5 tablespoons (60–75ml)
 olive oil
3 tablespoons (45ml) lemon juice
pepper

Soak bread with crusts removed in water. Squeeze out surplus liquid and blend bread with cod's roe. Still blending, slowly add onion, squeezed through a garlic press, olive oil, lemon juice and pepper to taste.

◣ POTTED SHRIMPS OR PRAWNS ◢

6 PEOPLE

8oz (225g) butter
1lb (450g) shrimps or small
 prawns

pinch of cayenne
pinch of nutmeg
salt and pepper

Clarify butter by melting in pan until frothy, then chill in glass jug in fridge until the top clear butter can be seen separated from the sediment, which should be discarded. Heat clarified butter again and add shrimps, a good pinch of cayenne and nutmeg (more if required) and season with salt and pepper. Heat almost to boiling point, then put into little pots and chill. Reserve some butter in pan and when butter in pots is solidified, pour on remaining just melted, but not too hot, butter to seal prawns completely from air. Serve with buttered, brown bread. Potted shrimps will keep for a couple of weeks in the fridge.

◣ HAM COOKED IN CIDER ◢

6 PEOPLE

There is no need to boil the ham, as cooking it covered in cider and finishing off with a glaze makes a deliciously moist, tasty and good looking joint. Take a very sharp knife to carve thin slices.

3lb (1.4kg) piece of gammon,
 approx
2 tablespoons Dijon mustard
1 tablespoon of marjoram or
 oregano

cider
cloves
3 tablespoons dark brown sugar
neat orange squash or juice

Soak gammon in water for a couple of hours and dry off. Preheat oven to 350°F, 180°C, gas mark 4. Take skin off gammon, leaving fat. Mix mustard with herbs and rub all over, avoiding fat. Place joint in a roasting pan just big enough to fit it and pour in 1in (2.5cm) of cider. Cover with foil and cook for 40 minutes a pound. 30 minutes before the end of cooking time, remove from the oven. Score the fat each way diagonally to make diamond shapes and stick a clove in each corner. Mix sugar to a spreadable paste with the orange squash or juice and spread over the fat. Return to the oven uncovered to finish cooking. Remove from the roasting pan and allow to cool completely before packing.

The cooking juices can be reserved and used for soup. Try cooking some lentils, draining them and blending with the cooking juices, or blend with a tin of haricot or flageolet beans.

◼ TURKISH LAMB ◪

6 PEOPLE

boned shoulder of lamb (4–5lb/ 1.8–2.2kg)
2 cloves garlic, cut into slivers

salt and pepper
3 sprigs rosemary
4oz (125g) butter, oil or dripping

Stuffing

1oz (25g) butter
1 large onion
4oz (125g) lamb's liver (finely chopped)
4oz (125g) thick grain rice, boiled and dried

1 dessertspoon parsley
1 dessertspoon marjoram
1½oz (40g) stoned raisins
2 tablespoons chutney
1 egg
salt and pepper

Preheat oven to 350°F, 180°C, gas mark 4. Make small incisions in outer skin of boned shoulder and insert garlic. Season. Prepare stuffing by melting butter, sauté onion gently until soft, add liver and cook briskly for three minutes. Turn into bowl with rice, herbs, raisins, chutney and egg. Season with salt and pepper and stuff into lamb which should then be sewn up. Rub lamb all over with butter, oil or dripping, place rosemary on top, then roast in oven for 1½ hours.

◧ OLD ENGLISH PORK & RAISIN PIE ◩

10 PEOPLE

For the jellied stock

pork bones from the filling meat
2 pig's trotters or 1 veal knuckle
1 large carrot, sliced
1 medium onion stuck with
   3 cloves

10 whole black peppercorns
5pt (3l) water
bouquet garni

For the pastry

1¼lb (550g) plain flour
½ teaspoon salt
¼ teaspoon icing sugar

¼ teaspoon ground mace
8oz (225g) lard
⅓pt (200ml) water

For the filling

2¼lb (1kg) boned shoulder of
   pork or spare ribs, with approx
   ¼ fat to ¾ lean meat, finely
   chopped
8oz (225g) thinly sliced unsmoked
   bacon, chopped

1 teaspoon dried sage
½ teaspoon ground cinnamon
½ teaspoon grated nutmeg
½ teaspoon ground allspice
1 teaspoon anchovy essence
4oz (125g) stoned raisins

1 egg, beaten

First make the stock. Put all the ingredients in a large pan, bring to the boil and skim off any scum. Cover the pan and simmer steadily for 3–4 hours. Remove the bouquet garni and strain off the stock into a clean pan and boil down until about ¾pt (450ml) stock is left. Season to taste. Cool and skim off any fat. The stock will set to a delicious firm jelly.

Preheat oven to 400°F, 200°C, gas mark 6. To make pastry, sieve the dry ingredients into a large mixing bowl. Bring the water and lard to the boil, then pour it quickly into the dry ingredients and mix rapidly together to a smooth dough with a wooden spoon or electric beater. Leave the dough covered in a warm place until it cools just enough to handle easily, but do not allow it to go cold or it will disintegrate. Cut off about a quarter of the dough and keep warm and covered for the lid. Put the remainder into a hinged pie mould, or a 7 or 8in (18–20cm) round cake tin with a removeable base. Quickly and lightly mould the pastry up the sides of the tin leaving no cracks.

Mix together all the ingredients for the filling except the raisins. Pack one-third of this meat mixture into the pastry case and cover with half the raisins. Repeat once more, then finish with the remaining meat mixture, letting it round up above the rim of the tin a little.

Roll out the remaining dough for the lid. Brush the edges of the pastry case with a little beaten egg and press the lid on firmly. Trim the edges and cut a hole in the centre of the lid. Use any surplus pastry to decorate and make a rose to cover the central hole. Brush all over with beaten egg and put in the oven. After 30 minutes, reduce the oven temperature to 325°F, 160°C, gas mark 3 and cook for a further 1½ to 2 hours. Cover the pie with foil or brown paper if it is browning too quickly. Remove the pie from the oven and leave to cool a little. Take it out of the mould or tin and brush the sides with beaten egg. Return to the oven for about 10 minutes to colour. When the pie is lightly brown all over, take out of oven, lift off rose and pour into the hole some of the warmed jellied stock using a small funnel or a cone of cardboard. This stock will fill any gaps left by the shrinking meat and will turn to jelly when cold. Replace the rose and allow to cool for at least 24 hours before serving.

As alternative fillings, other meat can be used to make raised pies using the same method. Try using chicken and ham, turkey and ham, duck, or veal and ham with or without a hard-boiled egg.

◧ ROAST MEATS & SAUCES ◨

Cold meats make delicious picnic food, but are easier to eat if cut into strips and served in a sauce, or included as part of a salad. Below are a few suggestions for sauces and other ingredients to add to the cold meats.

Ham – goes well with a mustard vinaigrette or devilled sauce.

Lamb – try blending a cucumber with some yoghurt and chopped mint, or instead of a cucumber a bunch of watercress.

Pork – goes well in ratatouille, which can be blended if required, barbecue sauce, or try a sweet and sour sauce (see below).

Chicken/Turkey – delicious with fruit sauces (see below), barbecue sauce or a curry sauce such as Coronation Chicken (see below).

Sweet & Sour Sauce

1 onion
1oz (25g) butter
¼pt (150ml) cider
2¾fl oz (75ml) water
1 dessertspoon demarara sugar

1 tablespoon (15ml) Worcestershire sauce
1 tablespoon fruit chutney
2 tablespoons arrowroot

Chop onion and fry in a little butter until translucent, then add all other ingredients except arrowroot and simmer for 15 minutes. Blend arrowroot with a little water, add and cook for a further minute. Season with salt and pepper to taste.

Apricot Chicken

6 boned chicken breasts or 6–12
   drumsticks
4 tablespoons runny honey
1oz (25g) melted butter

1 tablespoon (15ml) soy sauce
1 large tin apricots
juice and rind of a lemon

Preheat oven to 325°F, 160°C, gas mark 3. Skin chicken. Mix honey, melted butter and soy sauce in casserole dish, blend the apricots with their juice and add to honey mixture. Grate in the rind of a lemon and add the juice. Add the chicken, turning to coat well and marinate overnight in the fridge. Cook for 1 hour or until chicken is cooked through. Place chicken on serving dish, allow to cool thoroughly, then spoon on a little sauce.

Coronation Chicken

1 onion
whole cloves
1 carrot
1 stock of celery

3–3½lb (1.4–1.6kg) chicken
6 peppercorns or good sprinkle
   pepper
salt

For the sauce

1 onion
2 tablespoons (30ml) olive oil
3 teaspoons curry powder
2 teaspoons tomato purée
½pt (300ml) chicken stock or red
   wine
1 bayleaf (optional)

salt and pepper
¼pt (150ml) double or whipping
   cream
2 tablespoons apricot jam
½pt (300ml) mayonnaise
chopped parsley

Peel the onion, halve and stick with cloves. Peel carrot and chop roughly. Chop celery roughly. If you have any leek tops, broccoli stalks or other vegetables, chop roughly and add for flavour. Place them all in a large pan, lay the chicken on top and just cover with water. Add seasoning, bring to the boil and simmer gently for 45 minutes or until cooked through. Remove chicken and if using stock for the sauce instead of wine, reduce stock to just ½pt (300ml). Strain and keep.

To make sauce, peel and chop onion finely, heat oil in pan and sauté onion until golden. Stir in curry powder and tomato purée and add wine or stock a little at a time, stirring constantly. Add bayleaf and seasoning, bring to boil and simmer gently for 10 minutes. Take off heat, allow to cool and remove bayleaf.

Meanwhile, whip cream until stiff. Either remove chicken from bone, skin and cut into bite-sized pieces, or skin and joint into portions. It is easier to eat at a picnic if cut into pieces so no knife is needed. Mix jam into mayonnaise, stir in stock and finally fold in cream. If you have cut chicken into pieces, mix most of the sauce with the chicken, retaining a little to pour over the top for a smooth surface, otherwise pour over the joints in dish. Sprinkle with chopped parsley.

Mango Chicken

6 cooked and boned chicken
   breasts
2 ripe mangoes

1 teaspoon (5ml) or more
   vinegar/lemon juice to taste
basil, finely chopped

Skin breasts. Peel mangoes and put all the pulp into a blender, scraping off skins and stones. Blend and add vinegar or lemon juice. Arrange breasts on serving dish and pour over sauce. Decorate with basil.

Other ingredients to add to cold meat

Gherkins; capers; celery; apple; chutney; spring onion; peaches (with ham or chicken); cheese; green beans; small potatoes; olives.

◣ TUNA & PASTA SALAD ◪

6 PEOPLE

8oz (225g) pasta shells
1 bunch spring onions
8oz (225g) seedless green grapes
½ cucumber

2–3 crunchy green apples
3 tablespoons mayonnaise
1 tablespoon (15ml) lemon juice
2 × 14oz (400g) tins tuna

Cook the shells in plenty of salted boiling water until just cooked, then run under cold water and drain. Do not allow to go soft. Chop spring onions finely, drain tuna, wash and halve grapes, chop cucumber and, at the last minute, apples into bite-sized pieces. Mix mayonnaise and lemon juice and toss all ingredients together in a bowl. Do not add the apples if preparing the pasta a day in advance as they will go soft. Add the morning of the picnic.

Some alternative ingredients are: grated cheddar cheese; celery; red peppers; tinned sweetcorn; peas.

◨ POTATO SALAD ◪

6 PEOPLE

1¾–2¼lb (800g–1kg) new
  potatoes
1 bunch spring onions
2 tablespoons mayonnaise

1 tablespoon (15ml) vinaigrette
  (or lemon juice)
salt and pepper

Cook the new potatoes in salted boiling water. When cooled slightly, peel and slice into the serving bowl. They are much easier to peel when cooked. Chop the spring onions finely and add to potatoes. Mix together well mayonnaise and vinaigrette, season with salt and pepper and pour over potatoes, mixing to coat them all over. Just mayonnaise or just vinaigrette can be used according to taste, and a whole variety of ingredients can be added to this basic salad, as suggested below.

Additional suggested ingredients are: fresh mint; finely chopped hard-boiled egg; chives; cubes of garlic sausage; gherkins; green beans; watercress; apples (dip apple slices in the lemon juice first to prevent browning); rollmop herrings; celery.

◨ COLESLAW ◪

6 PEOPLE

½ medium white cabbage
1 bunch spring onions or ½
  spanish onion
1lb (450g) carrots
4oz (125g) cheddar cheese
1 crisp apple

2oz (50g) walnuts
2oz (50g) currants
3 tablespoons mayonnaise
1 tablespoon (15ml) vinaigrette
  or orange/lemon juice
salt and pepper

Shred the cabbage finely, chop onions finely, peel and roughly grate the carrots. Chop cheese into small cubes, core and chop apple into small pieces and mix all these ingredients together with the walnuts and currants in a serving bowl. In a cup, mix the mayonnaise with the vinaigrette or lemon/orange juice to thin, and season to taste. When you have the consistency you prefer – you may like more mayonnaise – mix in thoroughly with the ingredients.

Optional extra ingredients for coleslaw are: cauliflower florets; broccoli florets; red or green pepper, finely chopped; peeled and pithed orange segments; banana slices; sliced mushrooms.

If you wish to make the coleslaw a one-dish meal, meat or fish can be added. Suggestions are: well-drained and flaked tuna fish; chopped sausages; chopped Frankfurters; chicken pieces; tinned or fresh salmon; prawns or shrimps; bacon pieces.

◣ EASY MAYONNAISE ◪

MAKES HALF PINT

Do remember that all foods with raw eggs should be kept chilled until eaten, so give this priority in the coolbox or pack with ice and insulate well with newspapers.

1 egg yolk
1 whole egg
olive oil

1 tablespoon (15ml) wine vinegar
salt and pepper

Put egg yolk, whole egg and 1 tablespoon (15ml) olive oil in processor and whizz for about 20 seconds. Add vinegar and whizz again, then add oil through the top in a slow trickle, keeping the processor running throughout. When the mayonnaise is thick enough for your requirements, stop and add salt and pepper to taste.

This mayonnaise can be flavoured as required. Some suggestions are: chopped herbs for a green mayonnaise; chopped capers and/or gherkins for a tartare mayonnaise; chopped egg and tomato (skinned); chilli chopped (or chilli sauce), tomato purée and Worcestershire sauce for a spicy Mexican mayonnaise.

Add the above ingredients little by little to required taste.

◧ TOMATO & DILL MAYONNAISE ◨

Delicious with fish, this mayonnaise also goes well with potato salads and hard-boiled eggs.

4 tomatoes
1 clove garlic
1 egg and 1 yolk
3 tablespoons (45ml) white wine
   vinegar

1 teaspoon sugar
1 teaspoon mustard powder
½pt (300ml) sunflower oil
2 tablespoons chopped dill
salt and pepper

Put tomatoes in bowl, cover with boiling water, leave for a few minutes then drain, cool under cold water, peel and de-seed. Peel garlic and crush. Blend all ingredients except dill and tomato until smooth, season with salt and lots of pepper, then add tomatoes and dill and blend again.

◧ TOMATO SALAD ◨

6 PEOPLE

A favourite way of serving tomatoes, this recipe brings out all their flavour. It goes well with cold meat and green salad and is a perfect accompaniment to meat loaf.

8 tomatoes
bunch of spring onions or ½
   Spanish onion
several sprigs of fresh basil

2 level teaspoons sugar
salt and freshly ground black
   pepper
4 tablespoons (60ml) vinaigrette

Pour boiling water over tomatoes, leave for 2 minutes then peel and slice finely. Trim and chop spring onions finely, then basil. Spread half the onions over the bottom of the serving dish, then half the sliced tomatoes, going in circles from the outside in and slightly overlapping each other. Sprinkle with half the basil and sugar and season with salt and pepper. Repeat, then drizzle vinaigrette all over salad and leave to sit for an hour or so. For ease of packing, a smaller dish can be used and the salad layered up more.

◪ PEACH & HAZELNUT SHORTCAKE ◪

6 PEOPLE

6oz (175g) butter
4oz (125g) caster sugar
2 eggs
1lb (450g) self-raising flour
4oz (125g) hazelnuts
2oz (50g) brown sugar

4 large peaches (or nectarines)
2 dessertspoons (20ml) lemon
juice
1 heaped teaspoon ground
cinnamon

Preheat oven to 350°F, 180°C, gas mark 4. Cream together butter and sugar, then beat in eggs and flour. Toast hazelnuts until brown through, then rub off skins and chop roughly. Mix or process with sugar but retain rough texture. Peel and slice peaches fairly thickly. Grease a deep 9in (22.5cm) sandwich tin evenly and fill with just under half the shortcake mixture. Sprinkle on hazelnut and sugar mixture, then arrange sliced peaches on top leaving ½in (1.25cm) around the edge. Sprinkle peaches with lemon juice and cinnamon. Arrange over the top the remainder of the shortcake mixture. Do not smooth down as the mixture will spread itself and looks good crumbly rather than smooth. Bake for 35 minutes. If you can make this just before leaving, it is even more delicious warm, served with cream.

◪ SUMMER FRUIT CAKE ◪

Fruit cake is always popular and goes surprisingly well with cheese – try serving it with a slice of Stilton. If not finished at the picnic, it will make a good stop-gap for the journey back, or tea on arrival home!

6oz (175g) butter
6oz (175g) caster sugar
3 eggs
9oz (250g) flour, half plain, half
self-raising

2oz (50g) glacé cherries
grated rind and juice of ½ lemon
8oz (225g) mixed dried fruit
1 level tablespoon granulated
sugar

Preheat oven to 325°F, 160°C, gas mark 3. Grease and line a 7in (18cm) round cake tin. Cream butter and caster sugar together until light and fluffy. Beat in the eggs, one at a time. Fold in flour, halved glacé cherries, lemon juice and dried fruit. Pile the mixture into the cake tin and distribute evenly with a level surface. Sprinkle granulated sugar on the top and bake for 1¾ hours. When cooked, a skewer inserted in the middle should come out clean.

ROMANTIC
PICNICS

ROMANTIC PICNICS

Anthony Trollope depicts a picnic intended for the advancement of romance in *Can You Forgive Her?*, published in 1864–5. He sets his scene in the Norfolk seaside town of Yarmouth, where the picnic is planned by widowed Mrs Greenhow and her suitor, Mr Cheesacre:

> Yarmouth is not a happy place for a picnic. A picnic should be held among green things. Green turf is absolutely an essential. There should be trees, broken ground, small paths, thickets, and hidden recesses. There should, if possible, be rocks, old timber, moss, and brambles. There should certainly be hills and dales, – on a small scale; and above all, there should be running water. There should be no expanse. Jones should not be able to see all Greene's movements, nor should Augusta always have her eye upon her sister Jane. But the spot chosen for Mr Cheesacre's picnic at Yarmouth had none of the virtues above described. It was on the seashore. Nothing was visible from the site but sand and sea. There were no trees there and nothing green; – neither was there any running water. But there was a long, dry, flat strand; there was an old boat half turned over, under which it was proposed to dine; and in addition to this, benches, boards, and some amount of canvas for shelter was provided by the liberality of Mr Cheesacre.

Given this unpromising scenario, the picnic was not a great success, especially in matters romantic. Mr Cheesacre is upstaged in a whole series of ways by his intimate friend, Captain Bellfield:

> There was a great unpacking, during which Captain Bellfield and Mrs Greenhow constantly had their heads together in the same hamper. I by no means intend to insinuate that there was anything wrong in this. People engaged in unpacking pies and cold chicken must have their hands in the same hamper.

Separated from the widow at the picnic table, Mr Cheesacre attempts to make up for lost ground in the dancing on the seashore: 'The sands in question were doubtless compact, firm and sufficiently moist to make walking on them comfortable; but they ruffled themselves most uncomfortably under the unwonted pressure to which they were subjected. Nevertheless our friends did dance on the sands; finding, however, that quadrilles and Sir Roger de Coverley suited them better than polkas and waltzes.' But even in this endeavour, Mr Cheesacre was cheated, for another guest arrives to ask them to break up the party, late hours being dangerous to her daughter, Ophelia. 'At this moment the delicate Ophelia was to be seen under the influence of the music, taking a distant range upon the sands with Joe Fairstairs' arm round her waist.'

The marine picnic drew to a close. Mr Cheesacre had failed in his venture, though Ophelia and Joe Fairstairs clearly felt that the unpromising environment of the Yarmouth foreshore did hold romantic possibilities.

◩ FILO PACKAGES ◪

2 PEOPLE

1 orange	*4 spring onions*
2in (5cm) ginger root	*1 carrot*
1 dessertspoon (10ml) oil	*¼lb (120g) fine green beans*
1 dessertspoon (10ml) soy sauce	*16 sheets filo pastry*
1 breast of duck	*oil – preferably sesame or walnut*

Grate orange rind, crush half ginger in garlic press and mix these with oil and soy sauce in oven-proof dish. Peel and pith orange and reserve half the segments, squeezing the rest into the dish with the oil mixture. De-bone and skin duck breast and roll in marinade. Leave for several hours, turning occasionally.

Preheat oven to 350°F, 180°C, gas mark 4. Carefully remove eight of the longest leaves from the spring onions and reserve. Chop the rest in half lengthways and then into 1in (2.5cm) long pieces. Thinly slice and chop into small pieces the remainder of the ginger. Add these to the duck, cover with foil and cook in oven for 30 minutes; the breast should still be pink. Meanwhile, peel carrot, cut in half lengthwise and into 2in (5cm) lengths and trim beans. Cook carrot for 5 minutes in boiling water, add beans and cook for a further 2 minutes, then refresh under cold water. Cut into matchsticks. Drop the eight spring onion leaves into the boiling water for two minutes and refresh them in cold water. Take duck from oven and leave to cool.

Take a sheet of filo pastry, brush with oil, place a second sheet on top, brush with oil and fold sheets in half to form a square. Slice the duck breast thinly and cut into bite-size pieces. Put ⅛ of the spring onion and duck in the middle of the pastry, top with an orange segment and ⅛ of the beans, first dipped in the duck cooking sauce. Fold up each of the corners to make a bundle, making sure there is no gap to spring a leak. Tie up the bundle gently with blanched spring onion leaf. Repeat to make eight parcels, then move to baking tray and brush outside of parcels with oil. Bake for 15 minutes or until golden brown. Allow to cool completely before covering or packing.

An alternative filling for the parcels is ham slices, then pieces of chicken breast cooked to pink, topped with Gruyère or Emmental.

◪ QUAILS' EGGS IN NESTS ◪

2 PEOPLE

These nests look wonderful and are easy to make though fiddly. The effect is well worth the effort.

6 quails' eggs
2 slices white bread
oil
½ teaspoon turmeric
½ teaspoon paprika

1 teaspoon parsley, finely chopped
1 box cress
1 tablespoon mayonnaise
*   flavoured with lemon juice*

Preheat oven to 400°F, 200°C, gas mark 6. Put eggs into a pan of cold water, bring to the boil, boil for 1 minute and then leave eggs under running cold water until cool. Use a fluted cutter to cut two 2in (5cm) circles from bread. Brush both sides with oil and fit into a bun mould sheet. If you have two bun mould sheets, put the second on top to keep the bread in the mould. Bake for about 10 minutes until crisp and golden, lift out and cool on rack. Heat teaspoon of oil with the turmeric and turn two eggs into it over a gentle heat until deep gold all over. Sprinkle two more eggs with paprika and speckle the last three with finely chopped parsley. Line the nests with a little cress, the lemon mayonnaise and then the eggs.

◪ PRAWN & COURGETTE KEBABS ◪

2 PEOPLE

1in (2.5cm) root ginger
1 tablespoon (15ml) oil
1 tablespoon (15ml) sherry
1 tablespoon (15ml) runny honey
2 tablespoons (30ml) lemon juice

2 tablespoons (30ml) soy sauce
1 medium courgette
10 or 12 king prawns or other
*   large-size prawns*

Peel ginger and crush a little at a time in a garlic crusher into a small bowl. Add all the ingredients except courgette and prawns and mix well. Peel prawns and leave to marinate in the mixture for a few hours.

Preheat oven to 350°F, 180°C, gas mark 4. Top and tail courgette and, using a wide blade potato peeler or slicer, slice thin strips the whole length of the courgette. Roll each prawn in a strip of courgette and thread on to a skewer. Brush with the marinade and bake in oven for 15 minutes, turning and brushing with marinade occasionally. Take the remainder of the marinade to dip into on the picnic.

◤ MUSTARD POUSSIN ◢

2 PEOPLE

1 poussin
3 teaspoons Dijon mustard
2 teaspoons mixed herbs

salt and pepper
1oz (25g) butter

Preheat oven to 350°F, 180°C, gas mark 4. With a teaspoon or fingers, gently loosen the skin each side from the breast and thigh, keeping the skin intact. Mix together the herbs and mustard, salt and pepper and push this mixture into the pouch between skin and flesh, right down to the thigh and all over the breast area. Cut the butter into three and put a knob into the same area on each breast and one into the centre cavity. Roast poussin for about 30 minutes, or until cooked and golden. Leave to cool completely before packing.

◤ BREADED LAMB CUTLETS ◢

2 PEOPLE

4 lamb cutlets, or 6 little rib
* cutlets*
4oz (125g) breadcrumbs

2 tablespoons thyme (or thyme
* and rosemary)*
salt and pepper
2 tablespoons Dijon mustard

Preheat oven to 350°F, 180°C, gas mark 4. Cut all meat and fat away from the rib bone where it will be held for eating. Mix breadcrumbs with finely chopped herbs and season with salt and pepper. Smear mustard all over the meaty end of each cutlet and press firmly into the breadcrumbs for an even cover all over. Place in a tin and cook for approximately 15 minutes, depending on size and how well done or pink you like your lamb.

◪ ARTICHOKE HEART PARCELS ◪

2 PEOPLE

2 globe artichoke hearts
1 small carrot
1 small courgette
6 French beans
1 dessertspoon broad beans
1 dessertspoon frozen peas

2 large and long slices of smoked
  salmon
1 tablespoon mayonnaise
  flavoured with a little lemon
  juice or herbs

Boil artichoke hearts in salted water until tender and set aside to cool. Peel carrot and place with courgette in boiling water until just tender but not soft, then remove and refresh under cold water. Add French beans, broad beans and then the peas to the pan of boiling water, cook until just tender, then refresh under cold water. Place artichoke heart in middle of smoked salmon slice and spread herb or lemon mayonnaise over the heart. Pile half the broad beans in middle, a little more mayonnaise, then top with half the peas. Cut courgette and carrot into thin sticks slightly longer than the height of the beans and peas and trim French beans to the same height. Stand around the broad beans on the artichoke heart leaning in at the top to make a wigwam shape. Keep together at the top with a dollop of mayonnaise and fold up salmon around vegetables. Secure firmly with cocktail sticks for travelling.

◪ STUFFED POTATOES ◪

2 PEOPLE

2 small potatoes
1 egg
2 spring onions

salt and pepper
1 tablespoon mayonnaise
black fish roe (optional)

Preheat oven to 350°F, 180°C, gas mark 4. Bake potatoes until cooked through, hard-boil the egg and finely chop with spring onions. Allow potatoes to cool a little, then cut off a small 'hat' from one end and carefully scoop out the potato from inside. Mix half potato with egg mixture, season with salt and pepper and add mayonnaise to taste. Gently stuff back into potatoes, replacing the little hats. Brush potato with oil and rub with salt and bake for a further 20–30 minutes until crisp. Allow to cool completely before packing, or wrap in foil and insulate with newspapers. Serve if required with black roe for dip.

◪ VEGETABLE PLATTER ◪

2 PEOPLE

The selection of vegetables for the platter is very much a matter of personal choice, though when choosing, try to pick different colours and textures. If you prefer vegetables cooked, do not let them get soft. They should be 'al dente', still crisp to bite. The suggestions below are some of many options.

Asparagus – tie in bundle and place stems down in boiling water with heads above water for 10 minutes, then lie down for further 10 minutes. An alternative way of cooking asparagus which gives a very nutty flavour is to preheat the oven to 350°F, 180°C, gas mark 4. Lie asparagus in roasting pan and dribble all over with olive oil. Season with salt and pepper and bake for 20 minutes turning occasionally.

Green beans – these should be cooked in boiling water for about 4 minutes. Plunge straight under cold water to refresh.

Mangetouts/sugar snap peas – cook in boiling water for several minutes and plunge in cold water to refresh.

Red and yellow peppers – cut in half and grill, outer side up, until charred. Peel and cut into matchsticks.

Tomatoes – use raw cherry tomatoes, or if not cherry, the smallest available. Otherwise large tomatoes cut into quarters or halves and sprinkled with salt, pepper and chopped basil.

Courgettes – sliced into sticks and eaten raw or boiled for a minute or so, then plunged into cold water.

Mushrooms – button mushrooms raw.

Cauliflower – raw and divided into small one-bite florets.

Carrots – scrub skins, or if old, peel, cut into sticks and have raw.

Potatoes – peeled new potatoes, boiled in minted water until just cooked, but not soft. If larger than bite size, cut in halves or quarters.

Chicory – divided into individual leaves.

Artichoke hearts – boiled in salted water until tender, then cut in two or four.

Spring onions – peel carefully, and trim green leaves.

Celery – cut into sticks.

Cucumber – cut into sticks.

Radishes – leave some leaves on, wash and trim bottoms.

Arrange the prepared, chosen vegetables on a platter around a bowl of mayonnaise, aïoli or cream cheese-based dip, flavoured as required.

◩ AÏOLI ◪

1 clove garlic
1 egg yolk
¼pt (150ml) olive oil

1 tablespoon (15ml) lemon juice
salt

Peel garlic and crush, then add egg yolk and blend until smooth. Add oil slowly as for mayonnaise, thinning occasionally with some lemon juice. Season with salt and add remaining lemon juice to taste.

If you do not have time to make aïoli, blend a crushed garlic clove and some lemon juice well into mayonnaise. Other flavourings for mayonnaise that go well with vegetables include a little Dijon mustard and lemon juice, chopped herbs, tomato purée, and tahini to taste.

◩ DIPPED FRUIT ◪

2 PEOPLE

strawberries
grapes
cherries

2oz (50g) plain chocolate
1 egg
icing sugar

Leave a little stalk on the fruits, wash and dry well. Line a small tray or plate with baking parchment or greaseproof paper. Melt chocolate in a double boiler, or a bowl over a saucepan of simmering water. When just liquid, remove from heat, take each strawberry and cherry by the stalk and dip into the chocolate to coat half the fruit, then place on greaseproof paper to dry. Separate the egg white from the yolk and sieve a little icing sugar on to some greaseproof paper. Dip each grape half into the egg white, wait a few minutes for it to dry a little, then roll in the icing sugar to give a frosted look. The strawberries are also effective frosted. Arrange fruit, stalk upright, in a little glass dish or individual patty cases.

◩ STRAWBERRY SHORTBREAD ◪

2 PEOPLE

4oz (125g) plain flour
pinch of salt
1 tablespoon caster sugar
3½oz (100g) butter
2–3 tablespoons double cream

1 drop vanilla essence (not
    flavouring) if required
8oz (225g) strawberries (or
    raspberries)
1 teaspoon icing sugar, if required

Preheat oven to 400°F, 200°C, gas mark 6. Butter a baking tray. Sift flour, salt and caster sugar into a bowl. Dip your fingers into the flour and using your fingertips, work the butter into the flour lightly until blended. Divide mixture into four and shape into circles or hearts on the baking tray. Prick all over with fork and bake for 15 minutes or so until very light brown (just turning). Turn out on to wire rack and cool. Beat double cream with icing sugar and vanilla essence if required. Halve the strawberries. Place two shortbread bases on serving dish, spread with two-thirds of the cream, and top with halved strawberries. Spread remaining cream on top of strawberries and lay shortbread circle on top. Dust with icing sugar if required.

The separate ingredients of this pudding can be taken to the picnic and assembled there if preferred.

◥ KISSES ◩

2 PEOPLE

1oz (25g) butter	*½ teaspoon baking powder*
1oz (25g) caster sugar	*2 teaspoons (10ml) lemon juice*
1 egg	*2 teaspoons grated lemon rind*
3oz (75g) plain flour	

Icing

1oz (25g) butter	*1 teaspoon (5ml) lemon juice*
2oz (50g) icing sugar	

Preheat oven to 350°F, 180°C, gas mark 4. Cream butter and sugar together, add egg, lemon juice and rind and beat well. Sift in flour and baking powder. Grease a baking tray, or line with baking parchment and drop on to it half teaspoons of the mixture. Bake for 10 minutes and leave to cool.

Meanwhile, cream butter and sift in half icing sugar, beating until creamy, then beat in lemon juice and finally the remainder of the sugar. When the kisses are cool, join two together with the icing.

Some alternatives are: instead of lemon rind and juice, try 1 good teaspoon of cocoa and 2oz (50g) of chopped walnuts (and dates if required). Use only 2oz (50g) flour and instead of lemon juice, use 1 teaspoon (5ml) of sherry and a drop of vanilla essence for the icing. Toasted almonds or hazelnuts can be used instead of walnuts and a good teaspoon of instant coffee, dissolved in 2 teaspoons of boiling water, instead of the cocoa. If using coffee, use the full 3oz (75g) flour.

FÊTES
CHAMPÊTRES

FÊTES CHAMPÊTRES

T he Oxford English Dictionary defines the *fête champêtre* as an outdoor entertainment, first entering our language in 1774. By this time, the Romantic Movement had made it fashionable to eat alfresco in beautiful surroundings. The role of the picnicker as noble savage did not, however, come naturally to Horace Walpole. In July 1770 he was invited to attend a party for Princess Amelia, sister of George III, at Stowe, the great landscape gardens in Buckinghamshire. He recorded the proceedings in a letter to George Montagu:

> On Wednesday night a small Vauxhall [the pleasure gardens on the south bank of the Thames] was acted for us at the grotto in the Elysian fields, which was illuminated with lamps, as were the thickets and two little barks [sic] on the lake. With a little exaggeration I could make you believe that nothing ever was so delightful. The idea was really pretty, but as my feelings have lost something of their romantic sensibility, I did not quite enjoy such an entertainment *al fresco* as much as I should have done twenty years ago. The evening was more than cool, and the destined spot anything but dry. There were not half lamps enough, and no music but an ancient militia-man who played cruelly on a squeaking tabor and pipe. As our procession descended the vast flight of steps into the garden, in which was assembled a crowd of people from Buckingham and the neighbouring villages to see the Princess and the show, the moon shining very bright, I could not help laughing, as I surveyed our troop, which instead of tripping lightly to such an Arcadian entertainment, were hobbling down, by the balustrades, wrapped up in cloaks and great-coats for fear of catching cold . . . I am a miserable walker, and the Princess though as strong as a Brunswick lion, makes no figure in going down fifty stone stairs. Except Lady Ann – and by courtesy, Lady Mary, we were none of us young enough for a pastoral. We supped in the grotto, which is proper to this climate as a sea-coal fire would be in the dog-days at Tivoli.

Lady Mary Coke, a fellow guest, noted in her journal that Walpole feared a chill from the grotto, and 'desired when we came back to the house a glass of cherry brandy by way of prevention'.

◧ ICED CUCUMBER & YOGHURT SOUP ◪

6 PEOPLE

1 bunch spring onions
3 tablespoons (45ml) olive oil
1 clove garlic, peeled and crushed
  with a little sea salt
1 teaspoon cumin
2 cucumbers

½pt (300ml) plain yoghurt or
  greek yoghurt
salt
juice of 1 lemon
pinch of cayenne
¼pt (150ml) milk, if required
chives

Slice spring onions, using most of the onion, and sweat in the oil with the crushed garlic and cumin for 8 minutes. Blend with roughly chopped, unpeeled cucumbers until a smooth purée is formed. Add yoghurt, salt, lemon juice and cayenne and blend, adding milk to produce required consistency. Chill. Adjust seasoning if necessary when very cold, before pouring into thermos. Serve garnished with finely chopped chives.

◧ GRAVADLAX ◪

6 PEOPLE

A delicious, and personally much preferred, alternative to smoked salmon, gravadlax is easy to make but requires two days to marinate, and a sharp knife to slice thinly.

2¼lb (1kg) tail piece of salmon
2oz (50g) sea salt
2oz (50g) granulated sugar

2 tablespoons dried dill
10 white peppercorns crushed

For the sauce

4 tablespoons French mustard
2 tablespoons caster sugar
2 egg yolks
12fl oz (350ml) olive oil

4 tablespoons (60ml) wine
  vinegar
salt and pepper
3 teaspoons dried dill
lemon juice

Fillet the salmon (or ask the fishmonger to do it), cutting through the middle along the backbone on both sides. Wipe fish on kitchen towel, but do not wash or rinse it. Check for small stray bones on both fillets using tweezers where necessary. Mix salt, sugar, dill and peppercorns. Rub mixture on to both sides. Place a third of the remaining mixture in a dish which will take the salmon snugly. Lay on it a fillet, skin side down. Sprinkle with another third of the mixture, then lay the second fillet skin side up. Sprinkle with remaining mixture and cover with cling film. Put another dish or board on top of this and weight it down. Marinate for at least 36 hours, turning every 12 hours. Serve thinly sliced, like smoked salmon.

To make the sauce, beat mustard, sugar and egg yolks together until smooth, then gradually add oil and vinegar, stirring briskly to keep the mixture smooth. Season with salt, pepper, dill and lemon juice to taste.

◪ EGG MOUSSE WITH DEVILLED SAUCE ◪

6 PEOPLE

Serve egg mousse in individual ramekins with sauce spooned over and decorated with a sprig of parsley or other herb, or from a mould with sauce dribbled over but not completely covering. Devilled sauce can also be used as a sauce for meatloaf, chicken or other cold meats.

$\frac{1}{4}$pt (150ml) white sauce
  1oz (25g) butter
  1oz (25g) flour
  2$\frac{3}{4}$fl oz (75ml) white wine,
    stock or water
6 hard-boiled eggs
$\frac{1}{4}$pt (150ml) mayonnaise
$\frac{1}{4}$oz (7g) gelatine

pinch cayenne pepper
$\frac{1}{2}$ teaspoon (2.5ml) anchovy
  essence (optional)
1–2 teaspoons (5–10ml)
  Worcestershire sauce
2 tablespoons (30ml) single
  cream

Devilled sauce

1 tin tomatoes
1 teaspoon sugar
$\frac{1}{4}$ clove garlic, crushed
3 tablespoons (45ml) oil
1 tablespoon (15ml) vinegar

2 tablespoons (30ml)
  Worcestershire sauce
1 tablespoon (15ml) tomato
  ketchup
1 teaspoon English mustard
salt and pepper to taste

Melt butter over low heat, add flour and stir, adding wine, stock or water slowly. Simmer for a few minutes to produce a smooth sauce. Cool. Chop eggs and mix with mayonnaise. Mix gelatine with a little cold water and warm until dissolved. Add to white sauce and stir into egg mixture. Season with cayenne, anchovy essence and Worcestershire sauce. When cold and thick, lightly whip cream and fold into mixture. Turn into mould or ramekins to set.

To make the sauce, simmer tin of tomatoes and juice until they can be mixed to pulp. Add sugar and crushed garlic. Take off heat and add other ingredients, mixing thoroughly. Cool and serve spooned around each serving of egg mousse or pour a layer on to each ramekin. Serve any extra sauce separately.

MOUSSES

The three mousses that follow can be made and served on their own, but quantities will need to be increased if this is the case. They look particularly appealing when combined and layered showing the pinks and greens. Use any combination according to your preference.

The salmon mousse should be made, then half the mixture packed into a cling film-lined mould. Chill to set, then pour on a layer of cucumber, sorrel or watercress mousse and again chill to set. Finally finish with another layer of pink salmon mousse.

For a special occasion, smoked salmon slices can be used to separate the layers. Cut the slices to fit the mould and lay on the set mousse before covering with the next layer. Cut a fish shape out of the smoked salmon to decorate the top.

◨ SALMON MOUSSE ◪

6 PEOPLE

This recipe can be used to make a colourful terrine with sorrel, watercress or cucumber mousse on p.89. To put the terrine together, follow the instructions above.

1 lemon
water
3 teaspoons gelatine
12oz (350g) cooked salmon

2 tablespoons mayonnaise
6oz (175g) fromage frais
salt and pepper

Whether serving as a colourful terrine or by itself, lightly oil the serving dish. If you will be turning the mousse out, also line the dish with cling film.

Squeeze lemon and make juice up to 4fl oz (100ml) with water. Sprinkle the gelatine on the lemon juice and warm until it has dissolved. Blend salmon, mayonnaise and fromage frais together. Tip into serving dish, season with salt and pepper and stir in gelatine. Set in fridge.

◪ CUCUMBER MOUSSE ◪

This mousse should be used to layer salmon mousse; it is not enough for six on its own.

1 packet gelatine
2 tablespoons (30ml) water
½ large cucumber
3oz (75g) Greek yoghurt
3oz (75g) cream cheese

2 teaspoons (30ml) vinegar
1 teaspoon sugar
1 tablespoon mayonnaise
salt and pepper

Sprinkle gelatine over hot water and dissolve fully – if the gelatine does not fully dissolve, heat gently. Roughly chop cucumber, sprinkle with salt and leave for half an hour before rinsing and draining on kitchen paper. Blend the cucumber with all the ingredients except gelatine and water. When gelatine is dissolved, pour into mixture and blend thoroughly. Pour into mould, lined with cling film and chill to set.

◪ SORREL MOUSSE ◪

6 PEOPLE

If you do not like the lemony flavour of sorrel, or it is unobtainable, use one bunch of watercress instead.

This recipe is designed to be used in a terrine with salmon mousse. If you wish to use it by itself, the quantity should be at least doubled.

1 good handful of sorrel leaves
4fl oz (100ml) chicken stock
3oz (75g) cream cheese
pinch nutmeg

salt and pepper
few drops of Tabasco
2 teaspoons gelatine
¼pt (150ml) double cream

Clean and trim sorrel and simmer gently in half the chicken stock until just cooked. Blend with cream cheese and seasonings. Sprinkle gelatine over remaining chicken stock and warm until dissolved. Add to sorrel and blend again. Whip cream and gently but thoroughly stir in sorrel mixture. Turn into a lightly oiled mould (lined with cling film if you will be turning it out to serve) and leave in the fridge to set.

◪ SALMON ◪

ALLOW 6oz (175g) PER PERSON

A whole salmon can be poached in a fish kettle or baked in the oven in foil.

To cook in foil

Preheat the oven to 275°F, 140°C, gas mark 1. Butter the foil generously and sprinkle with salt and freshly ground black pepper. Place the salmon in the centre of the foil, place a couple of bay leaves in the salmon with small knobs of butter, lemon slices and, if you have a bottle open, a couple of tablespoons of white wine. Fold up foil around salmon to make a loose parcel, making sure the joins are well sealed. Cooking times are: for 2lb (900g) salmon – 1½ hours; 3lb (1.35kg) – 2 hours; 4lb (1.8kg) – 2½ hours; 5lb (2.25kg) – 3 hours.

To poach

If the salmon is too large for your fish kettle, cut the fish in half and cook each half separately. When filleted, the fish can be put back together and covered with cucumber slices to hide the join.

Court Bouillon

2pt (1.2l) water	*2 celery sticks, chopped*
½pt (300ml) wine	*4 black peppercorns*
2 onions, peeled and chopped	*1 bouquet garni*
2 carrots, peeled and chopped	*pinch of sea salt*

Simmer ingredients together for 30 minutes, then allow to cool. Put salmon on the strainer in the fish kettle. Pour over enough Court Bouillon to cover the salmon. Put on the lid and bring to the boil slowly over a low heat. When the cooking liquor comes to the boil, remove at once from the heat and leave in the kettle until completely cool.

The Court Bouillon can be boiled down and used as stock for soup.

To fillet salmon

It is much easier to serve and eat salmon at a picnic if it has been skinned and filleted at home.

When salmon is cool enough, or cold, pull the fins from under the gills and slit the skin along the back up to the tail. Remove the fins from the back with bones attached. Carefully peel the skin away on both sides, using a sharp knife. Remove the two fillets from the bone on the first side in as large pieces as possible – but don't worry if they fall apart as they can be repositioned and stuck with a little mayonnaise later. Cut the backbone at the head and peel towards the tail, cutting as close to the tail as possible. Check there are no bones left in the flesh – tweezers can be useful. Carefully lift the bottom fillets on to the serving platter. If head, tail or bits of fillet have gone adrift, reposition them as they should be. Spread over the fillets a little mayonnaise – plain or herb or whatever you will be serving with the salmon – and then replace top fillets. Smooth more mayonnaise thinly over the top, disguising all joins and making the surface even. Cut a cucumber very finely and starting at the tail end, arrange overlapping slices to cover the fish. Chill.

If required, dissolve 2 tablespoons of gelatine in ¼pt (150ml) water with a good squeeze of lemon. Stir gelatine as it cools until syrupy and thick, then spoon over chilled fish as glaze.

◪ CUCUMBER STUFFED WITH PRAWNS ◪

6 PEOPLE

1½ *cucumbers*
6 *mint leaves, finely chopped*
2 *tinned pimentoes, chopped*
  (optional)

5fl oz (125ml) natural yoghurt,
  preferably Greek
¾lb (350g) shrimps
salt and pepper
paprika

Cut cucumbers widthways into 1in (2.5cm) lengths and carefully remove insides, leaving a small base. Chop insides finely, discarding pips if required. Add all ingredients except paprika and mix well. Standing cucumber lengths on their bases, pile with ingredients and sprinkle with paprika.

The filling and cucumber bases can be taken to the picnic separately and assembled on site.

◪ PRAWN SALAD ◪
with Basil & Mango Dressing

6 PEOPLE

12 *king prawns, cooked (more if*
  required)
½lb (225g) mangetout or sugar
  snap peas

1 *small radicchio lettuce*
½ *bunch curly endive*

Dressing

small handful of fresh basil leaves
1 *ripe mango, peeled and chopped*

2 tablespoons (30ml) lemon juice
4 tablespoons (60ml) oil

Shell and de-vein prawns, leaving tails intact. Steam or microwave peas until just tender. Drain and run under cold tap, drain.

For dressing, blend or process basil, mango and lemon juice until smooth. Gradually add oil while still blending until the mixture is combined and smooth.

The ingredients can be taken separately to the picnic and put together on to individual plates, or the lettuce and endive put on a serving dish, topped with mangetouts and prawns. The dressing should be taken in its own container and added just before serving.

This recipe is delicious with the addition of 2 tablespoons of pine nuts. Heat oil in small saucepan, add pine nuts, stir over low heat until lightly browned, drain on absorbent paper and leave to cool and sprinkle on top of mangetouts and prawns.

◣ MEAT ROULADE ◪

6 PEOPLE

12oz (350g) pork fillet	*1 clove garlic*
12oz (350g) turkey (or chicken) *breast fillets, skinned*	*4oz (125g) sliced ham* *olive oil*
large handful parsley	*lemon juice*
1 rounded teaspoon green *peppercorns*	*2¾fl oz (75ml) single cream* *(optional)*
2oz (50g) can of anchovy fillets	*salt and pepper*

Preheat oven to 300°F, 150°C, gas mark 2. Lay pork fillet on greaseproof paper and slice (but do not cut through) lengthways to open it out. With greaseproof on top, beat the meat as thin as possible. Slice and beat turkey fillets flat in the same way. Chop parsley, green peppercorns and anchovies finely and mix together with anchovy oil from can. Crush garlic into mixture. Keeping the pork fillet on greaseproof, smear with a third of the mixture, then cover with flattened turkey breasts. Top this with another third of the mixture, lay on slices of ham and cover with remaining mixture. Roll up carefully from the short side. Smear the bottom of a roasting pan with olive oil and place roll on this with the join (end of roll) underneath. Smear roll all over with lemon juice and olive oil and cover with foil. Roast for 1¾ hours, removing the foil after 1 hour. Remove from roasting pan to cool. At picnic, serve roulade in thin slices. If you require a sauce, bubble up pan juices to thicken slightly, cool until warm and mix in cream. Serve separately.

◣ CHINESE CHICKEN ◢

6 PEOPLE

6 chicken breasts (or turkey)
salt and pepper
3 bunches spring onions
6 sticks of lemon grass (if
unavailable use grated rind
from 2 or 3 lemons)
4in (10cm) ginger root

3 tablespoons (45ml) oil (sesame
oil is particularly good for this
recipe)
3 tablespoons (45ml) soy sauce
3 tablespoons (45ml) lemon juice
4 tablespoons (60ml) water
2 tablespoons fresh coriander (or
parsley if not available)

Debone and skin breasts, season with salt and pepper and chop into delicate, bite-size pieces. Trim spring onions and slice diagonally into 2in (5cm) pieces. Slice lemon grass into thin rings and peel and slice ginger into tiny slivers. Heat oil, add lemon grass and ginger, then cook pieces of chicken, turning constantly. Add liquids and cook a few minutes more, tossing the chicken pieces. Turn into serving dish and allow to cool. Sprinkle with finely chopped coriander before serving.

A clove of garlic can be added to the pan with the lemon grass and ginger if a stronger flavour is preferred. A further option is 2 tablespoons (30ml) of sherry.

◣ SPINACH & BOURSIN ROULADE ◢

6 PEOPLE

3oz (75g) butter
4oz (125g) frozen spinach leaves
4 eggs

2 tablespoons sour cream
salt and pepper
nutmeg

Filling

6oz (175g) Boursin flavoured
with herbs

3 tablespoons sour cream
2 tablespoons chives, chopped

Preheat oven to 375°F, 190°C, gas mark 5. Line Swiss Roll tin with greaseproof paper or baking paper and brush with oil. Melt butter and cook spinach until tender. Drain thoroughly and chop finely. Separate eggs and beat yolks in bowl, adding sour cream and then spinach. Mix well and add salt, pepper and a pinch of nutmeg. Whip whites until stiff, then stir one spoonful into spinach mixture before folding the rest in gently. Pour into tin and bake for 15–20 minutes until set and going golden brown. Lift out of tin with paper on to a teatowel or sheet of foil and leave to cool a little. Beat the Boursin with the sour cream until well mixed, add chives and spread evenly over the spinach roulade, not quite to the edges. Roll up carefully, and lift on to serving dish with the seam underneath.

A very colourful alternative is to use taramasalata (see p.63) instead of Boursin, or for dark green, pink and white, use cream cheese beaten smooth with a little milk as the first layer, with a layer of taramasalata on top, then roll up carefully.

◣ WHITE CHOCOLATE CHEESECAKE ◢

AT LEAST 6 PEOPLE

8oz (225g) shortbread biscuits
2oz (50g) melted butter
¾pt (450ml) crème frâiche or
  fromage frais

¼pt (150ml) double cream
12oz (350g) white chocolate
  milk chocolate or strawberries/
  raspberries to decorate

Crush biscuits and mix with butter. Line base of 10in (25cm) flan dish. Lightly whisk crème frâiche (or fromage frais) and lightly whisk double cream. Melt chocolate in a double saucepan and fold in crème frâiche and cream. Pour on to shortbread base and refrigerate overnight. Decorate with grated milk chocolate or strawberries/raspberries.

◣ RASPBERRY PAVLOVA ◢

6 PEOPLE

whites of 3 eggs
6oz (175g) caster sugar
1 teaspoon cornflour
1 teaspoon white wine vinegar

½pt (300ml) double cream
1lb (450g) fresh raspberries (or
  any other soft fruit), sorted and
  cleaned

Preheat oven to 275°F, 140°C, gas mark 1. Line a baking tray with baking parchment or oiled greaseproof paper and mark an 8in circle. Whisk egg whites with salt until stiff in large bowl. Add half sugar and whisk again. Mix cornflour and remaining sugar and fold into the beaten egg whites with a metal spoon. Stir in the vinegar gently. Spread the mixture over the marked circle, building up 'walls' around the edge and cook for 1¼ hours. Move meringue immediately to serving dish and leave to cool. Whip double cream until stiff. Take ingredients separately to picnic. Spread the cream over the meringue and pile the raspberries on top.

VEGETARIAN
PICNICS

VEGETARIAN PICNICS

The modern philosophy of vegetarianism, and of veganism, would have found little favour in medieval and sixteenth-century Britain. For the poor, their diet was often perforce vegetarian because meat and fish were expensive and scarce, especially in the winter months. Medieval monks, such as the Cistercians of Fountains Abbey, originally observed a meat-free diet as a sign of abstinence, although the strictness of their regime relaxed with time, allowing first 'two footed' animals like chickens, and later 'four footed' beasts to join the feast. Meat and fish formed a high proportion of a diet of the prosperous, so much so that it is believed Henry VIII and his courtiers suffered from scurvy and other vitamin-deficiencies because they ate so few fresh vegetables and fruit.

One family that early advanced the tenets of vegetarianism was the Yorkes of Erddig in North Wales. In 1749 Philip Yorke I, at the age of five, had 'chused chiefly to dine on vegetables', marking himself out as an oddity among his neighbours and trying the efforts of his cook. Not all the Yorkes were vegetarian: Thomas Jones, the butcher who supplied meat to Erddig in the 1790s, merited a portrait and verse in the famous series that hangs in the Servants' Hall. But the last squire of Erddig, Philip Yorke IV, reverted to his ancestor's taste, and impromptu picnics in the garden of bread, jam and cakes, were provided for National Trust staff as they organised the handing over of the house in 1973.

In 1847 a group of enthusiasts launched the Vegetarian Society, and within two decades it had a fair number of supporters, particularly in intellectual circles. One such supporter was Sir Walter Trevelyan of Wallington in Northumberland. He had decidedly modern tastes in vegetables, boiling nettles in place of spinach, and regularly gathering edible fungi for his breakfast. Augustus Hare in his diary recorded visiting Sir Walter and his wife Pauline for lunch at Wallington in 1861, 'which was as peculiar as everything else (Lady Trevelyan and her artists [Pre-Raphaelite friends] feeding solely on artichokes and cauliflowers).'

The first vegetarian cookery book, compiled by Martha Brotherton, was published in 1866; its range was severely limited, with few cheese recipes and none using rice. We hope the following ideas will be more inspiring!

◪ AVOCADO & ALMOND SOUP ◪

6 PEOPLE

2 leeks
1 tablespoon (15ml) oil
1pt (600ml) vegetable stock
salt and pepper
2 large or 3 small avocados

2oz (50g) ground almonds
¼pt (150ml) milk (optional – or
  add a little more stock)
lemon juice (optional)
small pot sour cream (optional)

Trim, clean and slice leeks and sauté in oil in a saucepan for a few minutes. Add stock, seasoning and simmer until tender. Cool slightly and blend. Peel and chop avocados roughly and add with ground almonds to the blender. When smooth, thin with milk, or a little more stock if preferred, to the consistency required. Taste and adjust seasoning or add a little lemon juice as desired. Serve hot or chilled and if desired, garnish with swirls of sour cream.

◪ TZATZIKI ◪

6 PEOPLE

1 cucumber
1pt (600ml) Greek yoghurt
2 cloves garlic

1 tablespoon fresh mint (or
  teaspoon dried mint)
½ packet gelatine (optional)
salt and pepper

Grate cucumber and squeeze in sieve to get rid of excess liquid. Mix into yoghurt with crushed garlic, tip into serving bowl and sprinkle with finely chopped mint. Season with salt and pepper. If you prefer the dip a little firmer, sprinkle half a packet of gelatine over 2 tablespoons of warm water. Stir well and heat to dissolve. Mix well into the tzatziki. Chill for several hours.

◪ GUACAMOLE ◪

6 PEOPLE

a small tomato
3 avocados
4 spring onions, finely chopped

1 tablespoon (15ml) lemon juice
1 tablespoon mayonnaise
2 drops Tabasco sauce

Scald tomato and peel, then chop into pieces. Reserving some lemon juice, blend all ingredients roughly and season to taste. Put into bowl and cover surface with remaining lemon juice and cling film to stop browning. Stir before serving.

◩ HOMMOUS WITH TAHINI ◩

6 PEOPLE

½lb (225g) chick peas
¼pt (150ml) tahini
½pt (300ml) lemon juice

1 garlic clove, crushed in olive or
    sesame oil
salt and pepper
paprika or cayenne

Soak the chick peas overnight, then boil for 1½ hours or until soft. Drain, keeping some of the liquid, then liquidise adding a little of the cooking stock as necessary. Blend in tahini and lemon juice alternately, a little at a time to taste. Too much tahini will overpower all other tastes so it is important to taste as you add. Mix in crushed garlic, salt and pepper and blend, using more cooking liquid if necessary to achieve the smooth texture necessary to be able to dip vegetables and bread. Turn into bowl and sprinkle with a little paprika or cayenne.

◩ MUSHROOM DIP OR PÂTÉ ◩

6 PEOPLE

4oz (125g) butter
1 bunch spring onions (or 1
    onion)
8oz (225g) mushrooms (flat or
    field have more flavour)

4oz (125g) single cream or Greek
    yoghurt (for dip) or cream
    cheese (for pâté)
1 teaspoon (5ml) lemon juice
nutmeg (optional)
salt and pepper

Melt butter and chop onions and mushrooms. Sweat onions in butter until nearly soft, then add mushrooms and sauté gently for a few minutes. Blend together with other ingredients roughly. Season to taste and if required add a pinch or so of nutmeg. Chill.

◩ PASTRY FOR QUICHES & SAVOURY TARTS ◪

FOR 6 INDIVIDUAL TARTS OR 8in (20cm) FLAN TIN

6oz (175g) plain flour
pinch of salt
2oz (50g) margarine

1oz (25g) lard
cold water

Preheat oven to 350°F, 170°C, gas mark 4. Sift flour and salt into bowl. Cut fat into tiny cubes and, using fingertips, lightly rub fat into flour. When it is crumbly, sprinkle over 2–3 tablespoons of water, gradually mixing it in until the dough forms a smooth ball that will come away clean from the bowl. Rest pastry in plastic bag in fridge for 20 minutes. Lightly grease tin or individual tins. Roll out pastry and line, pressing base and sides firmly. Prick with a fork all over and bake for 15 minutes. Add filling and bake for further 30 minutes, check after 20 if using individual tins.

For cheesey pastry, add 2oz (50g) grated cheese before the water and a pinch of dry mustard powder sifted with the flour.

For spicy pastry, add ½ teaspoon of paprika (or a pinch of cayenne) and sift with flour.

◩ TART FILLINGS ◪

FOR 6 INDIVIDUAL TARTS OR 8in (20cm) FLAN

Pear & Stilton Tart

4oz (125g) Stilton cheese
4 eggs
½pt (300ml) milk

pepper
1lb (450g) eating pears,
*   preferably Williams*

Preheat oven to 350°F, 180°C, gas mark 4. Crumble Stilton into pastry case. Beat eggs and mix with milk. Season with pepper and pour into pastry case. Bake for about 30 minutes, until filling almost set. Peel, core and slice pears lengthways. Remove tart from oven and lay pear slices around in a circle. Bake for a further 12 minutes or until pears are soft and cooked through.

Ratatouille

4oz (125g) aubergine
salt and pepper
1 onion
2 tablespoons (30ml) olive oil
1 clove garlic
6oz (175g) courgettes

8oz (225g) can tomatoes
½ teaspoon sugar
½ teaspoon dried basil
½ teaspoon dried thyme
sprigs of fresh thyme for
   decoration

The pastry case should be fully cooked as this filling is cooked and is ready to eat when the filling is spooned into the case.

    Slice aubergine and sprinkle with salt. Leave for 30 minutes, then rinse, dry and dice. Finely chop onion and sauté in the oil, then crush and add garlic and slice and add courgettes. Drain and chop tomatoes, and when vegetables are tender, add tomatoes, sugar and herbs, using a little tomato juice if needed and simmer for 10 minutes. Adjust seasoning and spoon into pastry case. Too liquid a filling will make the pastry soggy so discard any excess liquid. Decorate with thyme sprigs if available. No further cooking is required.

Basil & Tomato

1 onion
1 tablespoon (15ml) olive oil
1lb (450g) tomatoes
1 tablespoon (15ml) chopped
   basil

1 teaspoon salt
1 teaspoon sugar
Worcestershire sauce
Tabasco

Chop onion finely and sauté in oil until tender but not browned. Place tomatoes in a bowl and cover with boiling water. Leave several minutes, then discard water and peel tomatoes and chop roughly. Add half tomato mixture to onions with half basil, salt and sugar and simmer gently for 10 minutes. Add a couple of shakes of Worcestershire sauce and several drops of Tabasco. Taste and add more if required. Remove from heat, add uncooked tomatoes, discard any excess liquid, then spread over cooked pastry base, sprinkling with remaining half of basil. No further cooking is required.

◪ BROCCOLI & BLUE CHEESE ROULADE ◪

6 PEOPLE

1¼lb (550g) broccoli florets
1oz (25g) butter
4 eggs
2 tablespoons Greek yoghurt

salt and pepper
nutmeg
2oz (50g) grated Parmesan
cheese

Filling

1oz (25g) butter
1oz (25g) plain flour
4fl oz (100ml) milk

6oz (175g) Stilton or other blue
cheese

Preheat oven to 375°F, 190°C, gas mark 5. Line Swiss Roll tin with greaseproof paper or baking paper and brush with oil. Drop broccoli into boiling water and simmer until just tender; do not overcook. Drain and chop small, then sauté in butter for five minutes. Separate eggs and beat yolks in a bowl, adding yoghurt and then broccoli. Mix well and add salt, pepper and a pinch of nutmeg. Whip whites until stiff, then stir one spoonful into broccoli mixture before folding the rest in gently. Sprinkle Parmesan into the Swiss Roll tin, then pour in mixture. Bake for 15–20 minutes until set and turning golden brown.

When cooked, lift out of tin with paper on to a teatowel or sheet of tin foil and leave to cool a little.

Meanwhile melt butter, stir in flour and gradually add milk. Bring to the boil and add blue cheese, chopped roughly. Allow to cook for 4 or 5 minutes, gently combining all the ingredients. Allow to cool a little, then spread this mixture on to the roulade, not quite to the edges, and carefully roll up. Transfer to serving dish ensuring that the seam is underneath.

Spinach can be substituted for broccoli (see p.93). Other fillings which work well as stuffings in the roulades are raw mushrooms, shrimps, tomatoes, smoked salmon, chopped olives, ham, eggs and peppers. Chop small and mix with mayonnaise or cream cheese, flavoured with herbs as required. Ham or smoked salmon can be used in this way or used as a thin layer to separate the roulade from the filling and add colour.

◣ COURGETTE & CARROT ROULADE ◪

6 PEOPLE

2 eggs
3 medium-sized courgettes
20 mint leaves
2 medium-sized carrots

8oz (225g) cream cheese
mixed herbs, finely chopped
  (preferably fresh)
salt and pepper

Preheat oven to 375°F, 190°C, gas mark 5. Line Swiss Roll tin with greaseproof or baking paper and brush with oil. Separate eggs and beat yolks in a bowl. Grate courgettes and add to yolks with mint leaves. Whip whites until stiff, then stir a spoonful into courgette mixture before folding the rest in gently. Pour mixture into Swiss Roll tin and bake for 15–20 minutes until set and turning golden brown.

When roulade is cooked, lift out of Swiss Roll tin with paper on to a teatowel or sheet of tin foil to cool a little. Meanwhile, peel and grate carrots into the cream cheese with plenty of mixed herbs and seasoning. Spread carrot mixture on top of the roulade, not quite to the edges, and gently roll up. Transfer to serving dish, ensuring that the seam is underneath.

◣ SPICY BALLS ◪

6 PEOPLE

6oz (175g) chick peas
3oz (75g) split lentils
1 vegetable stock cube
½pt (250ml) water
8oz (225g) onion
2–3 tablespoons sesame oil (or
  other oil or butter)

2 teaspoons curry powder
1 teaspoon allspice
8oz (225g) mushrooms
4oz (125g) sesame seeds
1 egg (optional, will keep balls
  together better)

Soak pulses overnight. Preheat oven to 350°F, 180°C, gas mark 4. Simmer 30–40 minutes, until soft, in stock cube and water. Peel and chop onion and sauté in 2 tablespoons of oil until soft. Strain pulses (keep stock for soup) and add to onions with curry powder and allspice and stir over low heat for 5 minutes, then turn into blender. Sauté mushrooms in remainder of oil until soft and blend with mixture until smooth. Toast sesame seeds under grill until golden. If required for firmer balls, beat egg and mix into mixture before forming into balls and rolling in toasted sesame seeds. Bake in oven for 30 minutes.

◪ VEGETABLE PASTA ◪

6 PEOPLE

For best results pasta shapes, rather than ribbons (such as spaghetti and tagliatelle) should be used in this recipe. Choose from shells, bows or twists, either plain or flavoured with spinach or tomato. A mixture of white, green and red pasta shapes can be used for a colourful and attractive dish.

6oz (175g) pasta shapes	*1 bunch spring onions*
6oz (175g) cauliflower	*1 tablespoon mayonnaise*
6oz (175g) broccoli	*1 tablespoon (15ml) lemon juice*
2 courgettes	*2 tablespoons (30ml) vinaigrette*
6oz (175g) peas	*salt and pepper*
4oz (125g) baby sweetcorn	*6oz (175g) strong Cheddar*
2–3 carrots (young ones if	*3oz (75g) sunflower seeds*
available)	*2 tablespoons chopped parsley*

Boil pasta shapes in well-salted boiling water until just cooked, then rinse with cold water and drain well. Cut the cauliflower and broccoli into small florets, slice the courgettes and steam or boil for just a few minutes: they should not be allowed to overcook and go soft. Cook the peas and sweetcorn the same way. Slice the spring onions and carrots, mix the mayonnaise, lemon juice and vinaigrette together and toss with all the vegetables and pasta shells in a bowl. Season well. Grate cheese and mix into pasta. Toast the sunflower seeds evenly under the grill and sprinkle with the chopped parsley over the pasta. If the sunflower seeds are left too long in the pasta they will eventually go soft, so if you are making the dish the day before, reserve the seeds and sprinkle on before leaving.

It is very important that the vegetables are not overcooked. They should still be crunchy to avoid giving the vegetable pasta a soggy texture. You may prefer to add the cauliflower and broccoli raw.

Alternative or additional ingredients are: croûtons; toasted almonds, hazelnuts or pine nuts; chopped chives; fresh or dried herbs; haricot beans; fresh broad beans; green beans; mangetouts; raw mushrooms; cherry tomatoes; celery; asparagus; red peppers; apples; grated Parmesan.

◪ VEGETABLE & SOYA LOAF ◪

6 PEOPLE

4oz (125g) soya beans	*4oz (125g) almonds*
1 vegetable stock cube	*8oz (225g) onions*
½pt (300ml) water	*2 eggs*
8oz (225g) carrots	*2 teaspoons celery salt*
8oz (225g) parsnips	*1 good handful coriander*
2oz (50g) sunflower seeds	*1 good handful rocket*

Soak beans overnight. Preheat oven to 350°F, 180°C, gas mark 4. Simmer beans for at least 45 minutes or until soft in stock cube and water. Peel and chop carrots and parsnips; add carrots to stock, simmer for last 15 minutes of cooking and add parsnips for 10 minutes. Toast sunflower seeds and almonds evenly under the grill, peel and chop onion and beat eggs. Blend all ingredients together, not letting the mixture get too smooth. Line a loaf tin with non-stick baking sheet or oiled greaseproof paper and bake for 45 minutes.

◪ THREE BEAN SALAD ◪

6 PEOPLE

Three bean salad can be made using whatever kind of bean you wish. For both taste and colour, it is good to include fresh green beans of some kind and kidney beans. If you wish to prepare the beans from dried, follow the instructions regarding soaking and cooking on the packet, drain and add to the salad.

8oz (225g) green beans	*1 bunch spring onions*
1 tin (432g) kidney beans	*vinaigrette (see p.44)*
1 tin (432g) flageolet beans (or	*1 handful chopped parsley*
cannellini, pinto or haricot	
beans)	

Top and tail green beans and cook in boiling water for 5 minutes or until just cooked. Chop in half, or to approximately matchstick lengths. Drain off liquid from the tinned beans and mix all three types together. Chop spring onions finely and add to beans. Toss in vinaigrette and sprinkle with parsley.

If you want to expand this salad and make it more colourful, try adding any of the following: sweetcorn, peppers, pimentoes, crispy bacon, halved cherry tomatoes, chopped Frankfurters or spicy sausage.

◣ CARIBBEAN SALAD ◢

6 PEOPLE

3 tablespoons rum
1½oz (40g) brown sugar
1 medium tin of corn, drained
1 large red pepper, chopped small
3 bananas, sliced

2 apples, peeled and thinly sliced
2 carrots, peeled and chopped
2oz (50g) cooked peas
3 tablespoons mayonnaise

Mix the rum and sugar and pour over chopped fruit and vegetables. Stir well to ensure all fruit is coated and does not go brown. Add mayonnaise and mix together.

◣ MEDITERRANEAN SALAD ◢

6 PEOPLE

5 tomatoes
1 green pepper
½ cucumber
6oz (175g) mozzarella or feta
    cheese

½ Spanish onion
1 avocado (optional)
4oz (125g) stoned black olives
4 tablespoons (60ml) vinaigrette
    (see p.44)

Pour boiling water over tomatoes, leave for two minutes, then peel and chop into quarters. De-seed and chop pepper, cube cucumber and cheese and slice onion finely. If using avocado, peel, slice and dip slices in lemon juice to stop them browning. Mix all ingredients together.

◣ BANANA RICE ◢

6 PEOPLE

5oz (150g) brown rice
2 lemons
5 tablespoons (75ml) oil
2 tablespoons demarara sugar
2 teaspoons curry powder

4 bananas
1 small red onion
4oz (125g) dry roasted peanuts
2oz (50g) dessicated coconut

Cook rice until tender but not soft. Cut lemons into quarters and blend with oil, sugar and curry powder until smooth. Drain and rinse rice under cold water and leave to cool. Slice bananas and mix in lemon dressing to prevent browning. Mix in rice, finely chopped onion, peanuts and lastly coconut. This will keep for a few days in the fridge.

◧ PEPERONATA ◪

6 PEOPLE

This is a mild, but tasty dish, which can be made hotter by leaving the pepper seeds in. It makes a colourful salad and acts well as a 'sauce' for meatloaf.

2 medium green peppers
2 medium red peppers
4 tablespoons (60ml) olive oil
1 medium onion, sliced

1 clove garlic, crushed
2 bay leaves
14oz (400g) can tomatoes

Preheat oven to 325°F, 160°C, gas mark 3. Cut peppers in half, remove seeds and membranes. Place peppers cut side down on oven tray. Bake in oven for 20 minutes. Cool slightly, peel and cut into 1in (2.5cm) strips. Heat oil in frying pan, add onion, garlic and bay leaves, and stir over medium heat for 5 minutes or until soft. Add peppers and crushed tomatoes. Bring to the boil, then reduce heat, cover and simmer for 15 minutes until soft.

For a brighter, red colour, use 4 red peppers and omit the green.

◧ FRUIT MOUSSES ◪

Fruit mousses are easy and quick to make and are delicious summer puddings. Any soft fruit can be used – raspberries, strawberries, red, white or blackcurrants, blackberries, mulberries, loganberries will all work with this recipe, or any mixture.

1lb (450g) soft fruits
4oz (125g) caster sugar
1 envelope powdered gelatine

4 tablespoons (60ml) water
½pt (300ml) double cream

Clean and pick through fruit, bruise it a little and sprinkle with sugar. Leave for an hour or so, turning every so often until the sugar is absorbed. Sprinkle the gelatine over the water and heat gently until dissolved. Sieve fruit and mix in gelatine. Whip the cream well and stir into the fruit purée. Whisk well and pour into individual ramekins or a serving dish. Decorate with whipped cream and fruit and mint leaves if available.

◥ APPLEY CAKE ◢

4oz (125g) butter or margarine　　　*1 egg*
4oz (125g) granulated sugar　　　*8oz (225g) self-raising flour*

Topping

¾lb (350g) cooking apples, peeled　*½ teaspoon ginger*
　and sliced　　　　　　　　　*½ teaspoon cinnamon*
2oz (50g) sultanas　　　　　　*2 dessertspoons brown sugar*

Preheat oven to 350°F, 180°C, gas mark 4. Melt fat over low heat. Take off heat and beat in granulated sugar, then the egg. Add the flour gradually, beating all the time. Grease a loose-bottomed 8in (20cm) tin. Spread two-thirds of the mixture in the tin. Mix apples and sultanas and spread over cake mixture. Sprinkle the ginger and cinnamon over the fruit. Pipe or place spoonfuls of the remaining cake mixture round the top and sprinkle the brown sugar over the surface. Bake for 45 minutes or until a skewer comes out cleanly.

MORE VITAL
INGREDIENTS

PICNIC CHECKLIST

Groundsheet
Rug
Tablecloth
Napkins
Cutlery
Plates and bowls
Glasses (if glass, wrap in
  tea-towel)
Mugs for soup and coffee or tea
Sharp knife
Bottle of water for spills and
  sticky fingers
Kitchen towel for the above

Salt and pepper
Corkscrew and bottle opener
Thermos of boiling water for tea
  or coffee
Teabags and coffee
Milk
Sugar
Candles in jam jars
Matches
Insect repellant and candles
Old plastic bags for dirty plates,
  cutlery, etc.
Bin bags for rubbish

ADVICE AND TIPS

Individual puddings look good and are easy to transport if kept in their pots or tins, ie mousses in ramekins or individual tarts or pies left in the patty tins for transporting.

If you are cooking a whole salmon to be the centrepiece, cook the salmon as normally. If you don't have a fish kettle large enough, cut salmon in half and cook each half separately, then fillet and put the halves back together again on the serving platter (see p.90). Covered with cucumber slices the salmon will look whole.

Paper plates and bowls are much easier to use as they do not break and go straight into the rubbish bag rather than home for washing up.

Choose food appropriate to style of picnic furniture – it is easier to eat with a knife and fork on a table than on a rug in a cramped sitting position. Use individual bowls or pots of things for such occasions and finger food.

Drinking vessels should be sturdy for rough picnics as they will fall over on uneven ground.

Frequent picnicker should keep basket primed with essentials, such as little salts, etc. so they are permanently ready and aren't forgotten.

Choose soups which can be hot or cold if the weather looks variable – vichyssoise, tomato, etc.

When you wish to serve cold meat, remember it is difficult to cut with a picnic fork, sitting at an awkward angle. It is much better to cut meat into strips and fold it into a suitable sauce or dressing. Shred green salad for the same reason.

Old plastic bags are very useful for storing dirty plates and cutlery to save everything getting messy on the way home.

Anti-midge candles are essential when picnicking by water and woodlands, and useful to have in any case.

Often, and especially if it is cold, a good solid pudding such as gingercake is more 'warming' and practical than a beautifully presented dessert.

Make a checklist of the food and drink you are taking and check it into the car – there is nothing so frustrating as leaving in the fridge the special dish you have made the day before!

Presentation

The presentation of picnic foods can be fun and make even a plain sandwich much more interesting.

Cut off crusts from sandwiches and arrange cress around piles of sandwiches for decoration.

Serve fruit salad from one of the fruits used – ie a scooped-out pineapple or, for a large group, water-melon looks more spectacular and fun than a dish and has the advantage of being unbreakable!

Individual tarts or slices of quiche are more interesting when arranged on a coloured paper napkin in a flat basket or platter.

Retain a few chopped fresh herbs from pasta, rice or any salad dishes or add some more to sprinkle over the top to make the dish look fresh and lively when serving.

Roulades and colourful terrines or mousses should be laid out with a few slices already cut to show the inside colours.

'Fruit bowls' make attractive containers – a scooped-out melon half is a good container to 'hang' prawns around with the mayonnaise or dip in the melon. Pineapples, oranges, or any fruit with a solid skin can be used as a decorative bowl.

Teabags?

PICNIC SITES
AT TRUST PROPERTIES

The National Trust does not allow picnics in the gardens of properties, but does provide picnic sites and in some cases facilities at a fair number of properties. For opening times and directions, please consult the National Trust Handbook.

No fires or barbeques are allowed on Trust property.

The properties listed below have a picnic area, benches or tables.

AVON

Dyrham Park, near Chippenham

BERKSHIRE

Basildon Park, Lower Basildon, Reading

CAMBRIDGESHIRE

Anglesey Abbey, Lode, Cambridge

Wicken Fen, Lode Lane, Wicken, Ely

Wimpole Hall and Wimpole Home Farm, Arrington, Royston (Hertfordshire)

CHESHIRE

Dunham Massey, Altrincham

Little Moreton Hall, Congleton

Lyme Park, Disley, Stockport

Quarry Bank Mill and Styal Country Park, Wilmslow

CORNWALL

Cotehele, St Dominick, near Saltash

Lanhydrock, near Bodmin

Trerice, Kestle Mill, near Newquay

Trelissick Garden, Feock, near Truro

CUMBRIA

Sizergh Castle, near Kendal
Fell Foot Park, Newby Bridge, near Ulverston

DERBYSHIRE

Sudbury Hall & Museum of Childhood, Sudbury

DEVON

Arlington Court, Arlington, near Barnstaple
Castle Drogo, Drewsteignton
Lundy, Bristol Channel
Lydford Gorge, The Stables, Lydford Gorge, near Okehampton
Overbecks Museum and Garden, Sharpitor, Salcombe
Parke, Haytor Road, Bovey Tracey

DORSET

Brownsea Island, Poole Harbour
Langdon Wood, Golden Cap Estate

GLOUCESTERSHIRE

Chedworth Roman Villa, Yanworth, near Cheltenham – picnicking in
  nearby woods

HAMPSHIRE

Hinton Ampner, Bramdean, near Alresford
Sandham Memorial Chapel, Burghclere

HEREFORD AND WORCESTER

Berrington Hall, near Leominster – picnic tables in car-park
Croft Castle, near Leominster – picnics in car-park only
Hanbury Hall, near Droitwich – picnics in car-park only

HERTFORDSHIRE

Ashridge Estate, Ringshall, Berkhamsted

KENT

Chartwell, Westerham
Emmetts Garden, Ide Hill, Sevenoaks
Ightham Mote, Ivy Hatch, Sevenoaks
Scotney Castle Garden, Lamberhurst, Tunbridge Wells
Sissinghurst Garden, Sissinghurst, Cranbrook

LANCASHIRE

Rufford Old Hall, Rufford, near Ormskirk

MERSEYSIDE

Speke Hall, The Walk, Liverpool
Formby, Victoria Road, Freshfield, Formby

NORFOLK

Blickling Hall, Blickling, Norwich
Felbrigg Hall, Norwich
Oxburgh Hall, Oxborough, near King's Lynn
Sheringham Park, Sheringham

NORTHUMBERLAND

Cragside, Rothbury, Morpeth
Hadrian's Wall and Housesteads Fort, Bardon Mill, Hexham
Wallington, Cambo, Morpeth
Allen Banks, near Bardon Mill

SHROPSHIRE

Attingham Park, near Shrewsbury
Wenlock Edge, Much Wenlock

SOMERSET

Montacute House, Montacute
Selworthy Church, Holnicote Estate, Exmoor
Bossington Car Park, Holnicote Estate, Exmoor
Dunster Castle, Dunster, near Minehead
Fyne Court, Broomfield, Bridgwater

STAFFORDSHIRE

Shugborough Estate, Milford, near Stafford

SUFFOLK

Ickworth, The Rotunda, Horringer, Bury St Edmunds

SURREY

Clandon Park, West Clandon, Guildford
Polesden Lacey, near Dorking
Runnymede, near Egham
Witley Common, Haslemere Road, Witley, Godalming
Hindhead, behind Hillcrest Café car-park
Ludshott Common car-parks

EAST SUSSEX

Bateman's, Burwash, Etchingham
Bodiam Castle, Bodiam, near Robertsbridge

WEST SUSSEX

Standen, East Grinstead

TYNE & WEAR

Gibside Chapel and Grounds, Rowlands Gill, Burnopfield, Newcastle-upon-Tyne
Souter Lighthouse, Coast Road, Whitburn, Sunderland

WARWICKSHIRE

Packwood House, Lapworth, Solihull – picnic site in avenue opposite house

WILTSHIRE

Avebury, near Marlborough
Stourhead Garden, Stourton, Warminster

NORTH YORKSHIRE

Beningbrough Hall, Shipton-by-Beningbrough, York
Fountains Abbey & Studley Royal, Fountains, Ripon
Mount Grace Priory, Osmotherley, Northallerton
Rievaulx Terrace & Temples, Rievaulx, Helmsley

WEST YORKSHIRE

East Riddlesden Hall, Bradford Road, Keighley

WALES

CLWYD

Chirk Castle, Chirk
Erddig Hall, near Wrexham
Country Park, Erddig, near Wrexham
Clywedog Heritage Trail, near Wrexham

DYFED

Stackpole Estate, near Pembroke

GWYNEDD

Penrhyn Castle, near Bangor
Plas Newydd, Llanfairpwll, Anglesey
Plas-Yn-Rhiw, Rhiw, Pwllheli
Porthor, Llyn Peninsula
Glan Faenol, Llyn Peninsula
Aberglaslyn Estate, Nantmor, near Beddgelert
Beddgelert Village
Carreg Farm, near Aberdaron

POWYS

Powis Castle, Welshpool

WEST GLAMORGAN

Aberdulais Falls & Historic Industrial Site, Aberdulais, near Neath

NORTHERN IRELAND

COUNTY ANTRIM

The Giant's Causeway, Bushmills
Carrick-a-Rede, near Larrybane
Cushendun Village

COUNTY DOWN

Castle Ward, Strangford, Downpatrick
Strangford Lough, Strangford
Murlough National Reserve, near Dundrum

COUNTY FERMANAGH

Florence Court, near Enniskillen
Castle Coole, Enniskillen
Crom Estate, Newtownbutler

COUNTY LONDONDERRY

Springhill, 20 Springhill Road, Moneymore, Magherafelt
Downhill Castle, Mussenden Road, Castlerock
Portstewart Strand, Portstewart

COUNTY ARMAGH

Ardress, Annaghmore
The Argory, Moy, Dungannon

RECOMMENDED
PICNIC SPOTS

The National Trust was set up to preserve places of historic interest or natural beauty, so all areas owned by the Trust have something to recommend them. The places mentioned below have a particular beauty, such as a wonderful view, or a lovely setting. They are not all easily accessible, so do consult Properties of the National Trust, the National Trust Handbook and a map before setting off. We would ask that you leave these places as you find them, with no hint that you have been there.

BUCKINGHAMSHIRE

Stowe Landscape Gardens, Buckingham – magnificent vistas and temples in these landscape gardens.

CHESHIRE

Helsby Hill, 20 miles west of Alderley Edge gives views of the mountains of North Wales and the Mersey and has an Iron Age hill-fort near the summit. Bickerton Hill at the southern tip of the Peckforton Hills also has views well worth the climb.

CORNWALL

With more than 110 miles of truly spectacular coastline, it is impossible to pick out particular stretches. All maps, however, mark places of exceptional scenic beauty or viewpoints.

CUMBRIA

Almost all the central fell area of the Lake District and the major valley heads and 24 lakes are owned or held on lease by the Trust. With such variety and beauty, it is difficult to pick out individual sites.

DEVON

Again, with 80 miles of coastline it is impossible to select individual sites, as the whole coast is worth exploring. Overbecks, near Sharpitor, Salcombe allows picnicking in the garden and has spectacular views over the Salcombe estuary. There are also many parks and woodlands to choose from; for details the Handbook should be consulted.

DORSET

At Golden Cap is the highest cliff in southern England. Named because of the yellow limestone and clumps of golden gorse, this viewpoint and the rest of the estate has 20 miles of paths for walkers, 2,000 acres including a $7\frac{1}{2}$ mile coastal footpath; anywhere on it is perfect for fit picnickers! For those less fit there are three miles of sandy beaches at Studland Beach and Nature Reserve, Studland Bay, Swanage.

ESSEX

Hatfield Forest, Takeley, near Bishop's Stortford – once part of the royal forests of Essex – offers chases and rides through the ancient woodland that are excellent for walks.

HAMPSHIRE

On the northern edge of the New Forest between Bramshaw, Cadnam and Plaitford, the Trust owns 1,400 acres of land with local grazing animals, walks and many sites for picnics.

ISLE OF WIGHT

The Trust owns more than 3,500 acres of the island, including beautiful chalk downlands with spectacular views such as Tennyson Down on the west of the island, where the Poet Laureate walked daily, St Catherine's Down and St Boniface Down on the south and Bembridge and Culver Downs on the east of the island. If you don't wish to climb with the picnic for the views, there are 15 miles of coastline such as Compton Bay, the popular bathing beach and St Helen's Duver, a wide sand and shingle spit.

LINCOLNSHIRE

Bellmount Tower in the landscaped park of Belton House, Grantham is a wonderful site with views over the house and park.

MERSEYSIDE

With the smell of pine trees and red squirrels, the 500 acres of dune, foreshore and pinewood between the sea and Formby make an attractive and interesting site.

MIDDLESEX

Osterley Park, Isleworth – the eighteenth-century pleasure grounds at Osterley Park include a Doric garden temple dedicated to Pan, making an ideal setting for picnics.

NORFOLK

Sheringham Park, Upper Sheringham – wonderful views of coast and countryside and walks through woodland, parkland and to the coast.

OXFORDSHIRE

Watlington Hill, on an escarpment of the Chilterns, and White Horse Hill, on the Berkshire Downs near Uffington, are ideal spots for picnics enjoying wonderful views. The beautiful rural area of the Buscot and Coleshill estates includes Badbury Hill and popular picnic areas at Buscot Weir and by the Thames, west of Buscot on the Lechlade Road.

NORTHUMBERLAND

Here is one of the most beautiful stretches of English coastline, with its numerous castles – some ruined, some in splendid repair, its miles of sandy beaches, links and sand dunes and its nature reserves and rocky offshore islands. All of these make spectacular backdrops for picnics.

SOMERSET

The Quantock Hills, in particular Beacon and Bicknoller Hills have magnificent views over the Bristol Channel and Exmoor and are wonderful areas for walking. On Exmoor, on the Somerset/Devon borders, the Trust has the Holnicote Estate with coastline, villages and hamlets and high tors. Any part of this can be recommended for walks and picnics.

SUFFOLK

Dunwich Heath, Saxmundham – high sandy cliffs giving great views, beach and heathland for nature walks. Ickworth Park, Bury St Edmunds – woodland and park walks, deer enclosure.

SURREY

At Hindhead, there are more than 1,400 acres of heathland and woodland making ideal sites for picnics and walks. The River Wey, a $19\frac{1}{2}$ mile stretch of waterway from Weybridge to Godalming Wharf, with its locks and weirs and towpath, makes for wonderful walks and a number of picnic sites, particularly beside the locks.

WEST SUSSEX

Black Down on the Surrey/Sussex border gives fine views to the South Downs and the English Channel. Cissbury Hill, near Findon, has the famous landmark Cissbury Ring on it and has views to Beachy Head and the Isle of Wight. Downland properties with spectacular views and walks include Newtimber Hill and Fulking Escarpment, as does Harting Down, near Petersfield.

WILTSHIRE

Stourhead, Stourton, near Warminster – this beautiful landscape garden provides the perfect setting for picnics.

WALES

CLWYD

Near Chirk Castle at Nantyr is a beautiful picnic site where you can enjoy magnificent views of the Llangollen valley. Erddig Country Park with extensive woods is perfect for walks and picnics.

GWYNEDD

The National Trust has many spectacular and varied locations in Gwynedd, including ones at Nantmor in the heart of Snowdonia, and the rugged and beautiful Llyn coastline.

NORTHERN IRELAND

With the woods and parklands, the Mourne Mountains and the dramatic North Antrim and attractive County Down coastlines, the picnicker is spoilt for good picnic spots.

INDEX